DEVIL'S ADVOCATES

DEVIL'S ADVOCATES is a series of books devoted to exploring the classics of horror cinema. Contributors to the series come from the fields of teaching, academia, journalism and fiction, but all have one thing in common: a passion for the horror film and a desire to share it with the widest possible audience.

'The admirable Devil's Advocates series is not only essential – and fun – reading for the serious horror fan but should be set texts on any genre course.'
Dr Ian Hunter, Reader in Film Studies, De Montfort University, Leicester

'Auteur Publishing's new Devil's Advocates critiques on individual titles... offer bracingly fresh perspectives from passionate writers. The series will perfectly complement the BFI archive volumes.' **Christopher Fowler**, *Independent on Sunday*

'Devil's Advocates has proven itself more than capable of producing impassioned, intelligent analyses of genre cinema... quickly becoming the go-to guys for intelligent, easily digestible film criticism.' *Horror Talk.com*

'Auteur Publishing continue the good work of giving serious critical attention to significant horror films.' *Black Static*

 DevilsAdvocatesbooks

 DevilsAdBooks

DEVIL'S ADVOCATES

THE TEXAS CHAIN SAW MASSACRE

JAMES ROSE

Acknowledgments

Given this book is all about family, the author would like to thank his parents, Pat and Barry Rose, for their sustained support and encouragement in all the creative endeavours he has undertaken. He would also like to thank his wife, Helen Rose, and brother, Christopher Rose, for their continued support and enthusiasm. Thanks also, once again, to John Atkinson at Auteur for his invaluable encouragement, support and critiques during the writing of this book.

First published in 2013, reprinted 2014 by
Auteur, 24 Hartwell Crescent, Leighton Buzzard LU7 1NP
www.auteur.co.uk
Copyright © Auteur 2013

Series design: Nikki Hamlett at Cassels Design
Set by Cassels Design www.casselsdesign.co.uk
Printed and bound by CPI Group (UK) Ltd, Croydon, CR0 4YY

British Library Cataloguing-in-Publication Data
A catalogue record for this book is available from the British Library

ISBN 978-1-906733-64-3
ISBN 978-1-906733-99-5 (e-book)

CONTENTS

TOBE HOOPER AND THE MAKING OF
THE TEXAS CHAIN SAW MASSACRE

Just like the many shifting facts that surround the development, production and financial problems of *The Texas Chain Saw Massacre* (1974), Tobe Hooper's biography is one of flux. Reading through a number of biographical commentaries, only one uncontentious detail becomes absurdly evident – that Hooper was born on 25 January, 1943 to Lois Belle and Norman William Ray Hooper. After this, Hooper's biography becomes a mire of stories and fictions, rumours and probable truth. For instance, a number of biographies indicate that Hooper undertook the Radio-Television-Film (RTF) programme at the University of Texas and would go on to study drama under Baruch Lumet.[1] Yet other biographies deny this[2] as do those that have worked with him. Sallye Richardson, the co-editor/assistant director of *The Texas Chain Saw Massacre*, has stated:

> Tobe's dad raised him in a hotel. He lived in the hotel as a kid and that's when he started making movies, he made little movies in the hotel. I guess 'cause he was bored. He was self-taught; there wasn't anything like film school… It was all instinct for Tobe – he learned by watching a lot of movies … (Jaworzyn, 2003: 115)

A number of other biographical sketches corroborate Richardson's comment by indicating that Hooper taught himself the craft of cinema from an early age. Yet, as Stefan Jaworzyn has suggested, even this seems to be uncorroborated:

> Few accounts of [Hooper's] childhood and adolescence contain the same facts. Some have him directing his first film at the age of three, being a professional child stage magician, having a father who owned a cinema where he spent all his time, a father with a hotel next to a cinema (where he spent all his time), a father who dealt in real estate and bought a whole block including a hotel and cinema … (ibid.)

What *does* emerge from these various biographies is the idea that the young Hooper was a film obsessive, watching as much cinema as he possibly could and, by doing so, become familiar with the language of film to the extent that he could replicate the narratives he had watched. Hooper himself has suggested that he made his first film at the age of five (but this is followed by a parenthesis in Jaworzyn's text to suggest that

Hooper has elsewhere also indicated that he made his first film at the age of nine) using the family's Super 8 camera. The subject of this is – perhaps predictably – as ambiguous as the rest of Hooper's biography. Some sources suggest it is an adaptation of Mary Shelley's *Frankenstein* while others indicate a pastiche of Roger Corman's series of Edgar Allan Poe adaptations, all (potentially) influenced by the lurid horror of the now infamous EC Comics.

By 1959 Hooper had directed a short entitled *The Abyss*,[3] then in 1963 a 10-minute short, *The Heisters*. Perhaps unsurprisingly, there is very little written about the film[4] but, two years after its production, Hooper's short warranted description in a brief side-bar in the June 1965 edition of the *Alcalde* (the University of Texas Alumni Magazine) which described it as 'a spectacular live-action comedy short' (Anon., 1965: 45). While Hooper continued to work on small-scale productions, two of his future associates had just met: Richard Kidd and Gary Pickle were working for KTVC, a local television station in Austin. Both left the station around 1966 to form a film company, Motion Picture Productions (MPP),[5] with the intention of making commercials and documentaries in and around the Texas area. A year before the formation of MPP, Hooper and Ron Pearlman (with the help of Robert A. Burns, whom Hooper had met at an impromptu party), were shooting a semi-documentary, *Down Friday Street* – a short film about the demolition of a building in Austin. Kidd would later see the film: 'that's when I wanted to get hooked up with Ron and Tobe. I thought it was great – these were the kind of guys we needed to be working with' (Jaworzyn, 2003: 18). The three met and Kidd invited them both to join MPP and become part-owners alongside himself and Pickle. One of their biggest ventures was a documentary about the folk singers Peter, Paul and Mary – *Peter, Paul and Mary: Song is Love* (1970). Using this film to develop and hone his film-making skills, Hooper would follow up *Song is Love* with what would become his debut feature film, *Eggshells* (1971).[6]

EGGSHELLS

With a budget estimated somewhere between $40,000 and $60,000, the funding for *Eggshells* was part private financing sourced by Hooper, with Film House providing the camera equipment, editing facilities and some of the crew.

Robert A. Burns describes the making of *Eggshells* as both *cinéma-vérité* and improvisation (ibid: 19) and so, in some respects, the narrative is one that potentially defies narrative description. On a surface level, it is a drama about a group of undergraduates sharing a house in Austin at the close of the 1960s. Within this basic construct a more complex narrative exists, infusing the unfolding drama with both supernatural and psychedelic qualities and imagery. Hooper himself describes it as:

> ... a real movie about 1969, kind of *vérité* but with a little push, improvisation mixed with magic. It was about the beginning and end of the subculture. Most of it takes place in a commune house. But what they don't know is that in the basement is a crypto-embryonic hyper-electric presence that managed to influence the house and the people in it. The presence has embedded itself in the walls and grows into this big bulb, half-electronic, half organic. Almost like an eye, but like a big light, it comes out of the wall, manipulating and animating. I've always described it as being a mixture of Andy Warhol's *Trash* and Walt Disney's *Fantasia*. (Anon., Austin Film Society)

When discussing *Eggshells*, Louis Black (2009) indicates that the film can be assessed from a number of perspectives – either a period piece that chronicles 1960s Austin, a minor entry in the psychedelic cinema movement, or, more simply, as the debut film from a future canonical director. As a *first* feature film, *Eggshells* offers an entry point into Hooper's dynamic as a film director, a position which Black takes when he identifies the film's cinematic elements: 'tell-tale camera movements, manipulations of POV, casually intricate cutting, and scenes that are mystifying and haunted' (Black, 2009). All these, as Black states, are the technical competences that Hooper would later put into more aggressive practice in *The Texas Chain Saw Massacre*. Hooper's own aforementioned description of the *Eggshells* inadvertently extends this observation as the director indicates both documentary techniques and the notion of improvisation – qualities that would have an influence on the *Chain Saw Massacre* shoot. In addition, Hooper's description indicates further similarities in that both films are preoccupied with an end of subculture, the predominate use of the domestic environment as the narrative's sole location and of how this domestic space has become subverted by an external agency.[7]

It was during the making of *Eggshells* that Hooper met Kim Henkel:

> Kim was one of the actors in *Eggshells*. That was how we met, and we worked
> together, Kim helped to develop it. Eventually we came to be collaborators on the
> script. Following *Eggshells*, we worked a year or so together and worked out the
> specifications on several projects; finally we came up with *Texas Chain Saw*. (Hooper,
> quoted in Jaworzyn, 2003: 27)

THE TEXAS CHAIN SAW MASSACRE

After the completion of *Eggshells*, Hooper and Henkel began to share and discuss ideas
for possible feature films, notably those that were located within the horror genre, as
both had observed that a number of independent films that were actual being shown
in cinemas (and therefore not only gaining an audience and [some] critical acclaim but
also making a return on investment) were horror films. In tandem with their discussions,
Hooper and Henkel approached the development of their ideas through watching
numerous horror films (Macor, 2010: 20), a quality which evokes Richardson's claim that
Hooper learnt his craft purely through observation and practice as opposed to having a
formal film education.

Reading through a range of critical texts, articles and reviews concerning the genesis of
The Texas Chain Saw Massacre, one of the most consistently repeated elements is that of
'The Plainfield Ghoul', the murderer and grave-robber Edward Gein (see also chapter
4). Within these texts, Gein is identified as the dominant influence upon Hooper and
Henkel when conceiving the idea of the story and during the writing of the script. This
is intriguing because Hooper has not identified Gein as the inspiration for the film.
Instead, he has stated that the inspiration came to him when he was in the hardware
department of large department store:

> I was in the Montgomery Ward's out in Capital Plaza. I had been working on this
> other story for some months — about isolation, the woods, the darkness, and the
> unknown. It was around holiday season, and I found myself in the Ward's hardware
> department, and I was still kind of percolating on this idea of isolation and such. And
> those big crowds have always gotten to me. There were just so many people to go

through. And I was just standing there in front of an upright display of chainsaws. And the focus just racked from my eyeball to the people to the saws — and the idea popped. I said, 'Ooh, I know how I could get out of this place fast — if I just start one of these things up and make that sound'. Of course I didn't. That was just a fantasy. (Snopes, 2007)

Hooper has also said that his childhood reading of the notorious EC Comics also had a direct influence upon the film:

They were absolutely frightening, unbelievable gruesome. And they were packed with the most unspeakably horrible monsters and fiends, most of which specialised in mutilation … I loved them. They were not in any way based on logic. To enjoy them you had to accept that there is a Bogey Man out there … I'd say they were the single most important influence on *The Texas Chain Saw Massacre*. (Jaworzyn, 2003: 30)

The process of writing the ideas into a screenplay was a nocturnal one: after finishing work at his daytime job, Henkel would go to Hooper's house for lengthy discussions. The products of these conversations were then converted into the working draft of a screenplay by Henkel who, sitting in Hooper's kitchen, would type out the details of the scenes and the dialogue. The first draft screenplay that pulled all of these ideas together – entitled *Leatherface* and consisting of 160 typed pages – was completed in approximately six weeks and subsequently reworked into a 100-page second draft (ibid.).

Having completed the script, Hooper and Henkel set about establishing the funding for the film: with three possible budgets – the highest of which was $60,000 – the pair met with a potential investor, Bill Parsley, via arrangement with noted screenwriter Warren Skaaren. At the time Skaaren was in the post of Executive Director of the recently formed Texas Film Commission, while Parsley was the Vice President for Public Affairs at Texas Tech University. After a successful meeting, a starting deal was struck with Parsley, who would invest $40,000 into the film's production. The remaining finances came from various sources, including Henkel's sister, Katherine, a friend of Parsley's, Austin attorney Robert Kuhn, and Richard Saenz, a friend of *Chain Saw* cameraman Daniel Pearl. Together, along with Marilyn Ann Burns, these four investors formed one of the film's two production companies, MAB. MAB would represent the investors and manage the business side of the film's production while the other, Vortex (set up by Hooper and

Henkel), would be the production company and therefore manage and represent the film-makers, cast and crew. Both MAB and Vortex stood to make 50 per cent of any financial profit *Chain Saw* made.

With the production companies established and the budget in place, Hooper and Henkel begin hiring the crew and auditioning. Looking back on his production experiences with *Eggshells*, Hooper approached Robert Burns, the designer of the *Eggshells* press kit, to act as art director, Wayne Bell as boom operator, Larry Carroll as editor, and Ted Nicolaou to record sound and his then-wife Sally for catering. Further partners were drawn into the production crew, including Daniel Pearl's wife, Dorothy, as make-up artist. As the hiring process gathered pace, Hooper and Henkel asked all those employed to defer their salaries in an effort to lower the film's initial production costs.

PRODUCTION

Principal photography on *Leatherface* began on 15 July, 1973. During the first week, the crew shot a number of interior and exterior shots but, upon the return of the dailies, some of the images were out of focus or too poorly lit to be seen. When Parsley and production manager Ron Bozman were informed of these problems, they intervened and temporarily shut the production down for eight days in order for the situation to be resolved and the remaining filming time better prepared for.

During this period, the film-makers tried to organise themselves. Members of the crew set-dressed the cannibal family's house, while Hooper and Henkel scouted for, and secured, further locations. In among this reorganisation, 'the producers… insisted that Hooper make and follow a shot list. The result was a three-and-a-half page typewritten chart' (Macor, 2010: 27). Filming resumed on 4 August and was scheduled to conclude twenty-four days later, with the cast and crew being allowed to take off only one day in every seven.

On the fourth day of the resumed shoot, the crew prepared for the Leatherface's first on-screen appearance – the murder of Kirk – while the following day, the house was prepared for Pam's entrance into the house and her subsequent impalement on the meat hook. Hooper's original intention was to have both strong and graphic imagery, ideally with a shot showing the hook piercing through Pam's chest in a spray of blood. Hooper approached Burns to construct a rig for the effect but, according to Burns, he talked the director out of it: 'subconsciously or not,' states Burns, 'people will wonder how you did the special effect, and it'll be much more effective without [it]' (ibid: 29). Once convinced, Hooper then asked for a rig that would allow Pam to be suspended upon the meat hook but Burns again refused, this time on the grounds of the implicit danger the gag implied for the actress, Teri McMinn. Eventually a harness was constructed by make-up artist Dottie Pearl comprising of flesh-coloured nylon stockings and a metal ring, allowing for her to be physically suspended from the meat hook.

By 18 August the crew were behind schedule, a situation compounded by further tensions on the set: John Dugan, the eighteen-year-old who played the cannibal family's Grandfather, refused to undergo any further application of the special-effects make-up to age him and Jim Siedow had only one day left on set due to prior acting commitments. This meant that the climax of Sally's torture – the evening meal with Leatherface and his brothers – had to be filmed over one long day. The actual experience of filming this sequence is perhaps as legendary as the film itself in the various fan circles that exist around the film: the sequence took a gruelling twenty-six hours straight to film and, although the sequence takes place at night, the sequence was shot during an intensely hot summer day. Blackout curtains were used to cover the windows in order to simulate nightfall and, while this worked, the curtains also intensified the stifling, still heat within the small dining room. This, combined with the studio lighting that was been used, created an intense heat – reaching around a 100 degrees – and the (real) animal carcass props and cooked food scattered across the dining table all began to smell. Compounding all this was a concern about continuity – none of the food could be moved from the table and the actors could not change their clothes, resulting in Siedow, Gunnar Hansen, and Edwin Neal all wearing the same clothes for the entire duration of the shoot:

> The decaying head cheese, rotting chicken corpses, and acrid body odour created an unholy stench in the small room. Dottie Pearl hovered just off camera so she could help Hansen navigate the space and touch up Dugan's and Burns' make-up during breaks. 'At one point,' says Pearl, 'I looked around and thought, 'We are truly living this thing. We aren't making it any more. We're living it.' (Macor 2010: 31)

Just as her character Sally endures the horrors of Leatherface and his family, so too did the actress in the 'infamous twenty-six hour filming sequence'.

As the cast and crew endured the filming of the dining room sequence, a further unexpected element had entered into the film's production: prior to filming, caterer Sally Nicolaou had reportedly 'helped herself to a marijuana crop growing in the backyard of the [cannibal family's] house and added it to her own Brownie recipe' (ibid.). The addition of this ingredient was not mentioned and soon those that had consumed the Brownies were stoned. Gunnar Hansen has commented 'I am convinced that's the reason we had the infamous twenty-six hour filming sequence ...' (Jaworzyn, 2003: 63).

Of all the actors within the film, Marilyn Burns had to perhaps undergo the most endurance – just as her character Sally would be tormented, beaten, tied down and humiliated, so too would Burns: Sally's torments begin when she is kidnapped by Cook who, having repeatedly hit her with a broom handle, bundles her into a sackcloth bag and throws her into his pickup. Unable to find a prop that did not look fake, actor Jim Siedow was instructed to use the real thing. To begin with he would pull the blows but this too looked fake. At the request of Burns, Siedow eventually ended up striking the actress for real. Burns then had to undergo Grandpa's repeated attempts to crack open her skull ('It was a sledgehammer – they took off the metal part but the handle was made of oak, so every time it hit my head it was killing me' [ibid: 38]), and then her eventual escape via jumping through a closed window:

> It's like 5.30am and nice and humid, and the sugar glass has crystallised into hard chunks and it's no longer crunchy but hard. And Tobe has this scaffolding there that's like six to eight feet [off the ground]. I asked, 'What's that for?' and Tobe says 'Oh this is where you jump out the window. You're going to climb up there and you're going to jump and we're going to throw the sugar glass in your hair when you hit the ground'. That's why I limped for the rest of the picture … (ibid.)

The final day of shooting took place on 2 September and was spent filming Sally's escape and Leatherface's insane chainsaw dance. Hooper had suggested to Hansen:

> … that he stamp his feet and gesture with the chain saw to show his frustration over Sally's escape in the back of the pickup. Hansen ad libbed the shot, stomping around and swinging the saw. Then Hooper and Pearl decided to move the camera 360 degrees around Hansen for a dizzying panoramic effect … at the end of the filming of this scene, which essentially marked the end of principal photography, Hansen hurled the chain saw into a nearby field and walked out of the frame. (Macor, 2010: 32)

POST-PRODUCTION

According to Macor, Kim Henkel expected the post-production of *Leatherface* to last no more than four weeks, a situation enhanced by the fact that editor Larry Carroll had been organising the dailies throughout filming and was, therefore, in a strong position to construct the rough cut. By October 1973 editing was well under way, with Carroll and Hooper working long hours in order to both edit and shape the film. While Hooper may have had creative freedom with *Leatherface*, he was still under pressure from his financiers, in particular from Bill Parsley who not only wanted the film finished quickly but was also pushing for a more censored final cut in an effort to get a younger film certification. While this seemed problematic because of the very nature of the film's subject matter, the insistence on a more conservative cut began to emerge as one of the film's many strengths – by editing to suggest and intimate, as opposed to simply showing the graphic events depicted within the narrative, the film's psychological intensity was exaggerated to even greater proportions.

The planned four weeks soon bled into months as Carroll continued to edit with Hooper and Hooper worked with Wayne Bell on the film's 'soundtrack' and sound design through many hours' jamming with improvised instruments. During this period of post-production, the film's title was dramatically changed. According to Carroll:

> Ron Bozman called in the midst of a poker game in Houston and had a good bit to drink, it sounded like, and I handed him off to Tobe. I was looking at Tobe and his eyes suddenly start to glow. He looks at me and says, 'The Texas Chain Saw Massacre'. My understanding was that Ron was telling people the stories and someone in the poker game came up with the title. (Macor 2010: 33)

While many of the production crew felt the shift in title was a positive one, Macor indicates that some were not as convinced, primarily because of the use of the State's name within the new title: at the time Texas was still haunted by the 1963 assassination of President John F. Kennedy and the 1966 shooting spree by Charles Whitman on the University of Texas campus (Macor 2010: 33–4). But, regardless of these concerns, Leatherface became The Texas Chain Saw Massacre, if only for the sheer exploitation quality this new title possessed.

As the editing process continued into the early months of 1974, Carroll left the crew to fulfil other editing obligations and was replaced by Sallye Richardson who, with Hooper, decided that the existing cut should be abandoned and the whole process started from scratch. This phase of the editing took place at screenwriter Bill Wittliff's premises and meant that editing could only take place after office hours. Consequently, Richardson would edit at night and sleep during the day (Jaworzyn, 2003: 73).

When the film was finally cut to Hooper's satisfaction, a distribution deal was struck with Bryanston Pictures who, on 4 September 1974, published a full-page advert in Variety to promote the film's forthcoming release. During the first four days of its initial screening in Texas, Chain Saw made $602,133 and received positive reviews. According to Macor's account, the film then went on to open in 105 cinemas in New York and at 45 in Los Angeles 'as well as select theatres in other states' (2010: 39). Perhaps unsurprisingly, the film received mixed reviews but continued to gain in popularity. The film's American success was compounded a year later when the film was screened at the London Film Festival and the Director's Fortnight at Cannes where it was met with critical acclaim. *Chain Saw*'s success would continue to grow when it was awarded the Jury's Special Prize at Avoriaz and further prizes at the Trieste and Antwerp Festival but, despite these successes with US audiences and global critics, the film would fall foul of the censors,[8] perhaps no more so than with the British Board of Film Classification.

ENDNOTES

1. For example, see Macor, 2010: 19.

2. 'Contrary to many accounts, Hooper did not attend the University of Texas in Austin' (Jaworzyn, 2003: 115). This statement is supported by Richard Kooris, the Director of Photography on *The Texas Chain Saw Massacre 2* who has stated 'I had known Richard Kidd for years, and of course Tobe – he started making films when he was really young, and down at MPP was where he got his education' (Jaworzyn, 2003: 17).

3. Jaworyn's text indicates a further biographical ambiguity here by stating in Hooper's filmography '1959, The Abyss (existence unconfirmed)' (2003: 126).

4. During the research for this chapter, very little could be found about *The Heisters* although Sallye Richardson does describe one scene: '[A man brings] out this giant pie, and this guy gets hit in the face with a pie that's about as big as a door…' (Jaworzyn, 2003: 15).

5. After graduating from the University of Texas, Sallye Richardson made a documentary about a children's mental health unit during the course of which she met Lou Perryman (younger brother of Ron) and they began working on a film together. The film was taken to MPP for post-production and, while working there, she met both Hooper and Ron.

6. In between directing *Peter, Paul and Mary: Song is Love* and *Eggshells*, Hooper acted in *The Windsplitter*, a low-budget exploitation film produced by David Ford. Hooper played one of the Wilson Brothers who take a disliking to the film's protagonist Bobby Joe Smith. While working on the film, Hooper would meet Jim Siedow who would go on to play the character of Cook in *The Texas Chain Saw Massacre*.

7. Subculture is bought to a symbolic end in *Chain Saw* as *Leatherface* brutally and systematically murders all but one of the trespassing hippie teens; both films use a normal domestic house as the site for their drama; the external/subverting force of the crypto-embryonic hyper-electric presence in *Eggshells* takes on a more politically threatening force in *Chain Saw* in the form of mechanical replacement of the workforce, a condition which results in the three brothers regressing into cannibalism in order to survive.

8. From 1974 onwards *The Texas Chain Saw Massacre* would be banned, for varying periods of time, in ten different countries: Australia, Brazil, Chile, Finland, Iceland, Norway, Singapore, Sweden, the United Kingdom and West Germany.

REFERENCES

The Austin Film Society, n.d. *Tobe Hooper's Eggshells.* [Online] (n.d.) Available at: https://www.austinfilm.org/sslpage.aspx?pid=1310 [Accessed 23 March 2012].

Alcalde, 1965. *Movies Produced in Texas.* [Online] (n.d.) Available at: http://books.google.co.uk/books?id=Z9IDAAAAMBAJ&pg=PA45&lpg=PA45&dq=the+heisters+tobe+hooper&source=bl&ots=BKP4R8z4vO&sig=0mDJLw5qdbe9HlKkmXUqjOvTAec&hl=en&ei=D42lTaL5OcW3-hAeBy5jQCQ&sa=X&oi=book_result&ct=result&resnum=10&ved=0CFAQ6AEwCTgK#v=onepage&q=the%20heisters%20tobe%20hooper&f=false [Accessed 23 March 2012].

Black, L., 2009. *Found Film: The Rehatching of Tobe Hooper's 1969 debut, 'Eggshells'* [Online] (n.d.) Available at: http://www.austinchronicle.com/screens/2009-03-13/754199/ [Accessed 23 March 2012].
Jaworzyn, S., 2003. *The Texas Chain Saw Massacre Companion*, London: Titan Books.

Macor, A., 2010. *Chainsaws, Slackers, and Spy Kids: Thirty Years of Filmmaking in Austin, Texas*, Texas: University of Texas Press.

Snopes, 2007. *The Texas Chain Saw Massacre* [Online]
http://www.snopes.com/movies/films/chainsaw.asp [Accessed 23 March 2012].

THE TEXAS CHAIN SAW MASSACRE AND THE BBFC

The succession of events surrounding the British censorship of *The Texas Chain Saw Massacre* is perhaps one of the longest in the annals of the British Board of Film Classification's (BBFC) history: lasting for nearly thirty years, the film's numerous submissions coincided not only with the tenure of two Secretaries, Stephen Murphy and James Ferman, but also the rise in the popularity of home video and the subsequent 'Video Nasty' campaign that emerged from it.

Before the film was submitted for classification at the then titled British Board of Film Censors, *Chain Saw Massacre* had already garnered a growing global reputation as being one of the most frightening films ever made. While this would seem to imply that such a film would be statured in scenes of graphic violence and bloodshed, this imposed status for *Chain Saw* came about from the very fact that there was so *little* violence and gore within it. Instead, audiences and critics were affected by the film's sheer emotional intensity, experiencing the horrific events, almost in real time, alongside protagonist Sally Hardesty. With the majority of films across all genres, such a reputation serves only to stimulate an increased audience curiosity and anticipation, potentially indicating larger audience figures (and therefore larger financial return) on the film than initially expected. Indeed, *Chain Saw* was eagerly anticipated but its most effective quality would impede its UK cinema release for nearly twenty-five years. As Ken Penry, Ferman's deputy at the BBFC at the time, has stated, *Chain Saw* 'was rather unique because it did not have particularly outrageous visuals; but it was so well made it had this awful impact all the way through' (Matthews, 1994: 252).

INITIAL SUBMISSION TO THE BBFC

As Stefan Jaworzyn states, on 28 February 1975 Stephen Murphy, then Secretary of the Board, sent an Internal Communication to his examiners:

> I saw last night *The Texas Chain Saw Massacre*. This appears to be a fictionalised documentary which bears every sign of being shot on 16mm and blown up to 35mm. It is a very good film, which we must take seriously. To my mind, although this is quite

frankly fictionalised, we are basically back to the kind of considerations we faced with *Manson*… The film differs from *Manson*, not only in technique, but also in the fact that, with the exception of one tiny incident where perversion is hinted at, it has no sexual content. I think there is relatively little blood around this film. Its documentary air makes it even more severe and even more distressing to watch than *The Last House on the Left*. (2003: 100)[1]

The Board's official screening of the film for possible certification would take place twelve days later on 12 March 1975 and was immediately rejected by the Examiners (one of whom was Ken Penry) on the grounds that it was sick and offensive and to sanction a film which features a prolonged attempt at murder as entertainment was 'to enter the Roman Circus stakes' (ibid). With its certification refused, Murphy wrote to the film's UK distributors Gordon Shadrick and John Daly of Hemdale International, stating:

I have to tell you that we do not feel we can offer certification to this film. I should make it plain we do not regard this is an exploitation piece: it is a film of considerable merit. The problem is, I think, our continuing worry whether studies in abnormal psychology are suitable for the public cinema. (ibid.)

Over the next two months, Murphy and Hemdale would exchange correspondence, each trying to define or reiterate its point of view on the film. Throughout these communications, Murphy indicates that the Board's censors were most disturbed by the 'appalling terrorisation of the girl and the violence, both physical and mental, to which she is subjected' and that he saw 'little hope' that the Board would change its decision (ibid). While the majority of the exchanges were negative, Murphy offered some hope – before resigning in May 1975, he suggested that Hemdale submit the film to the Greater London Council in an effort to obtain a GLC X Certificate.

SUBMISSION TO THE GLC

Murphy's suggestion to approach the GLC was an indication that the BBFC's refusal to certificate the film did not mean that it had received an outright ban – each local council within the UK licences the cinemas within its boundary. Consequently, this gives them the authority to change certificates, request further cuts or to ban a film from playing within their area's cinemas.[2] Such actions are rarely taken, with local councils usually concurring with the decisions made by the BBFC. Despite this, the GLC granted *Chain Saw* a certificate in August 1976 after Hemdale, following Murphy's advice, submitted the film to them. This meant that any cinema within the jurisdiction of the GLC could show the film if they so chose. This also meant that anybody in the UK could see the film *if* they could get to a cinema showing the film within the GLC area. Some commentators have indicated that this quality alone renders the BBFC's refusal to certificate *Chain Saw* as 'farcical and meaningless' (Powell, 2010).[3] With this small success, the film was submitted to other local councils, some of which allowed it certification.

By now the BBFC had a new Secretary, James Ferman. It is here that, as with many of the accounts surrounding the unique and plotted history of *The Texas Chain Saw Massacre*, the trials within its censorship history begins to have its contradictions.

Tom Dewe Mathews' account indicates that despite its restricted release, Hemdale still desired a BBFC certification in order to ensure a national release across the UK and 'so they retraced their steps to the BBFC's door two years later [1977], by which time James Ferman had become Secretary' (1994: 253).[4] Perhaps anticipating another rejection, Hemdale approached Ferman with a proposition: 'They asked me to come and work with their editor to see if we could make it more palatable' (Ferman, quoted in Mathews, 1994: 253).

Working together,[5] the editing team of distributor and censor soon realised that the film was, to some extent, censor-proof because it was not *individual* scenes that needed exorcising but the overarching *feel* of the film. Despite this, some scenes were cut, including some of the shots from Pam's meat-hook impalement and from Grandpa's attempts to kill Sally with a lump hammer. This cut version was then shown to the Board's censors and, as Ferman recounted, all said "it hasn't made any difference at all; it's exactly the same film. Taking out those moments of explicit violence has not helped'. The problem, they now realised, was psychological torture' (ibid.). Three years later, in 1980, Ferman would try and censor *Chain Saw* again 'but, once again, he was defeated by the fact that… Hooper always cuts away from the gaping evisceration and leaves the audience instead with the sound of an approaching chainsaw' (ibid.).

Mathews' account presents Ferman's approach to the film as one in which the censor is proactively and positively engaged[6] with the censorship process, all working in an effort to ensure a diversity of films are granted certification and consequential national release. In contrast to this potentially positive image are more negative accounts of Ferman's relationship to the film, in particular his *alleged* comments made after a particularly screening the film:

> After the film had been shown, uncensored, to members of the British Film Institute at the London Film Festival, Ferman got up on stage and, thinking he was among friends, said, 'It's all right for you middle-class cineastes to see this film, but what would happen if a factory worker in Manchester happened to see it?' (Anon., *The Ferman Chainsaw Massacre*)

Upon hearing Ferman's comment, the audience became predictably hostile due to its implications – that one sector of the British populace (who are implied to be 'educated' enough to understand the film) were able to watch the film 'unharmed' while another (uneducated) sector were not due to their inability to 'understand' or 'differentiate' from the content of the film.[7]

Jaworyn's account does not mention this incident at all and instead moves forward to October 1982. *Chain Saw* was by now being distributed by ITC Entertainment, who wrote to the BBFC asking if the film could be considered for a R18 Certification. This was an interesting approach as, if the certification were granted, the film could – technically – be released onto the burgeoning home video market as the R18 certificate means that such a certified video tape could be sold to the general public in legally licensed sex shops. No account indicates that the R18 was ever granted.

By May 1983 *Chain Saw* had changed distributor for a second time and was now being managed by Tigon, which again submitted it to the BBFC for certification. This time the film was viewed by three Examiners, one of whom was Ken Penry along with two female colleagues. At the end of the screening (according to Jaworzyn):

> [Penry] elected for passing the film R18 uncut, commenting '...this is still to me the most effective of all the horror films. I can admire the expertise with which it is made, but I still find watching it rather degrading experience with its persistent terrorising of

the girl… Now we have the Restricted 18 category this is the right classification for the film… it would mean that the sale of the video cassette would be restricted to licensed outlets only'. (2003: 103)

Both of Penry's colleagues felt that the film could be now released (with cuts, primarily to the scene in which Sally is humiliated and tortured) but their opinions of the film did differ: whereas one felt it to be sadistic and indulgent, the other, fearing she may 'be branded the office ghoul' admitted 'to enjoying this by now notorious movie. It is a classic piece of *grand guignol*, definitely not for the squeamish' (ibid.). Despite the Examiners' decisions, however, the film was again denied certification.

CHAIN SAW ON HOME VIDEO

Until 1984 there was no formal requirement that a home video to be released onto the UK sales market had to be certificated by the BBFC. Consequently, *The Texas Chain Saw Massacre* was released on home video at the end of 1981. While this seemed like an ideal way for the film to finally find its UK audience, a moral uprising was steadily taking place within the country, culminating in the 'Video Nasty' era.

The increasing popularity of the home video market, coupled with the lack of any regulatory constraints for these videos, meant that the UK video market was flooded with a range of international titles. These were often low-budget horror films, predominately from Italy and the US and included, among many other notorious titles, *Driller Killer* (Abel Ferrara, 1979) and *Cannibal Holocaust* (Ruggero Deodato, 1980). With their lurid and often violent promotional materials, these films soon became a cause for concern for some, due to the possibility that these violent and gory films could be seen by anyone who had a video cassette recorder in their home. The furore generated by these anxieties led to a moral crusade headed by Mary Whitehouse of the National Viewers and Listeners Association, and was amplified by the tabloid and broadsheet's 'moral campaign' to ban these films. *The Sunday People* was possibly the first newspaper to print an article on the subject, which was followed by a similar article in *The Daily Star* and then *The Sunday Times. The Times* printed an article by journalist Peter Chippendale entitled 'How high street horror is invading the home', with Chippendale providing a lengthy account of his experiences at a Manchester video fair, particularly in relation to the violent horror films that were available there. With such a succession of articles, a 'moral panic' was steadily rising. It took full form in *The Daily Mail*, which started its 'Ban the Video Nasties' campaign in June 1983 with an article entitled 'The rape of our children's minds'. Media interest in the Video Nasty was sustained in part by its own reporting and by the continued work of Whitehouse, who, at the 1983 Conservative Party Conference, presented a 'highlights' video of some of the more explicit content from the alleged Video Nasties. As a consequence, Conservative MP Graham Bright introduced a Private Member's Bill to bring about the regulation of video content, which led to the 1984 Video Recordings Act.

In response to this Act, the Director of Public Prosecutions (DPP) constructed a list of films he felt likely to be 'obscene' and therefore liable to prosecution under the Obscene Publications Act 1959. The Act itself meant that:

> … subject to certain exemptions, video recordings offered for sale or hire commercially in the UK must be classified by an authority designated by the Secretary of State. The President and Vice Presidents of the BBFC were so designated, and charged with applying the new test of 'suitability for viewing in the home'. (Anon., *About*, BBFC).

In total, seventy-two films appeared on the DPP 'Video Nasty' list. Yet despite its content and the implicit fear of campaigners that violent horror films have the potential to corrupt, *The Texas Chain Saw Massacre*, despite being repeatedly refused a theatrical certificate, never once appeared on the list. However, a direct consequence of the VRA meant that all films intended for video consumption at home now had to be submitted for reclassification (i.e. a film's video certificate did not always correspond with its theatrical rating). Once again, *The Texas Chain Saw* was submitted and, once again, it was refused classification.

FINALLY, RELEASED

James Ferman stepped down from his post as Secretary of the BBFC on 10 January 1999. His retirement was reported in *The Guardian* (28 March 1998), with the article indicating that Ferman resigned following the problems over certifying *Lolita* (Adrian Lyne, 1997) with an 18 certificate and that:

> … his position has been in jeopardy [for some time] since he moved to relax censorship of pornographic videos at the end of last year without consulting the Home Office. The decision brought a public dressing down from the Home Secretary, Jack Straw, and a return to previous guidelines on pornographic content. (Glaister, 1998)

Three months later, on Tuesday 16 March 1999, BBC News reported that after twenty-five years, *The Texas Chain Saw Massacre* was to be passed by the BBFC with no cuts and granted an 18 Certificate. This meant that, although the film had been actually screened at selected UK cinemas over those twenty-five years[8] it could now have a nationwide general release. To accompany the decision, the BBFC's President Andreas Whittam Smith and Director Robert Duval released a statement explaining why the film was finally being granted a certificate:

> There is, so far as the Board is aware, no evidence that harm has ever arisen as a consequence of viewing the film… For modern young adults accustomed to the macabre shocks of horror films through the 1980s and 1990s, *The Texas Chain Saw Massacre* is unlikely to be particularly challenging. (Anon., *Texas Chain Saw Massacre Released Uncut*, 1999)

In relation to the film's perceived violence, Smith and Duval define it within the statement as being implicit as opposed to explicit and that 'by today's standards its visual effects may seem relatively unconvincing'. Despite this, Smith and Duval give specific attention to one of the film's more notorious sequences, the sustained chase of Sally Hardesty. It is described in the statement as a half-hour pursuit of 'a defenceless and screaming female'.

> The board's conclusion, after careful consideration, [of the pursuit] was that any possible harm that might arise in terms of the effect upon a modern audience would be more than sufficiently countered by the unrealistic, even absurd nature of the action itself… It is worth emphasising that there is no explicit sexual element in the film and relatively little visible violence. (ibid.)

In August of the same year, the BBFC passed *The Texas Chain Saw Massacre*, uncut, for home video/DVD distribution across the UK. Just over a year later, *Chain Saw* was shown, uncut, on UK terrestrial television when Channel 4 broadcast it as part of their *FilmFear* season in 2000.

ENDNOTES

1. The film *Manson* to which Stephen Murphy refers to is the 1973 documentary directed by Robert Hendrickson and Laurence Merrick. *The Last House on the Left* (Wes Craven, 1972) suffered an equally long period as *Chain Saw* of repeated submission to the BBFC. The film was finally passed with an 18 (uncut) certificate in 2008 and is available on DVD retail.

2. 'The British Board of Film Censors was set up in 1912 by the film industry as an independent body to bring a degree of uniformity to the classification of film nationally. Statutory powers on film remain with the local councils, which may overrule any of the BBFC's decisions, passing films we reject, banning films we have passed, and even waiving cuts, instituting new ones, or altering categories for films exhibited under their own licensing jurisdiction.' (Anon., *About*, BBFC).

3. In the booklet that accompanies the Universal's 2002 Uncut Special Edition DVD release of *The Texas Chain Saw Massacre*, it is stated that 'individual councils were able to grant their own certificates allowing the film to be shown and as such, only Surrey, Sussex and Glasgow were deprived of the ultimate horror experience' (Anon, 2002: 7) suggesting that a number of cinemas across the UK granted certification in order for the film to be screened.

4. Jaworzyn indicates in his text that 'In January 1977 Gordon Shadrick wrote to James Ferman, informing him there had been an accidental cut of twenty-eight seconds to the print showing in London'. According to Jaworzyn, the missing footage was of Leatherface butchering Kirk. When bootleg videos of the film began to appear, a number of copies were struck from this 'cut' of the film, 'leading to the incorrect assumption that the film had been censored' (2003: 102).

5. This seems likely as *The Guardian* obituary for Ferman states that he 'conducted the business of the Board in a hands-on way' and states that he personally flew out to Hollywood to make twenty-four cuts to Steven Spielberg's *Raiders of the Lost Ark* (1981) to ensure a general UK release (Barker, 2002).

6. It does need to be stated that although Mathews does clearly describe Ferman's positive efforts to enable *Chain Saw*'s UK release, he does end his text by stating that 'if a film is censor-proof, though, the censorious do not question themselves. They merely remove the evidence of their failure' (Mathews, 1994: 253).

7.   Looking through the reams of research material concerning Ferman, very few make reference to the comments described in the text. A number of the UK broadsheets carried extensive obituaries upon Ferman's death (22 December 2002), none of which mention this incident.

8.   This was because 'individual local councils had been granted licences to show the film… most recently Camden in London [in 1998]' (Anon, *Texas Chainsaw Massacre Released Uncut*, 1999). Jaworzyn concurs with this limited release (2003: 105).

REFERENCES

Anonymous, 1999. 'Texas Chain Saw Massacre Released Uncut', *BBC News*, [Online] March 1999 Available at: http://news.bbc.co.uk/1/hi/entertainment/298009.stm [Accessed 23 March 2012].

Anonymous, *The Texas Chain Saw Massacre* (DVD Booklet), Universal Studios, 2002.

BBFC, n.d. *About*. [Online] (n.d.) Available at: http://www.bbfc.co.uk/about [Accessed 23 March 2012].

Barker, D., 2002. Obituary: 'James Ferman'. *The Guardian Online*, [Online] 27 December. Available at: http://www.guardian.co.uk/news/2002/dec/27/guardianobituaries.filmcensorship [Accessed 23 March 2012].

Glaister, D., 1998. Culture: Film: 'Controversial Ferman Quits as Chief Film Censor', *The Guardian Online*, [Online] 28 March. Available at: http://www.guardian.co.uk/film/1998/mar/28/filmcensorship. danglaister [Accessed 23 March 2012].

Jaworzyn, S., 2003. *The Texas Chain Saw Massacre Companion*, London: Titan Books.

Mathews, T. D., 1994. *Censored: What they didn't Allow you to See and Why: The Story of Film Censorship in Britain*, London: Chatto & Windus.

Melon Farmers, n.d. *The Ferman Chainsaw Massacre*. [Online] (n.d.) Available at: http://www. melonfarmers.co.uk/arbptcm.htm [Accessed 23 March 2012].

Powell, S., n.d. 'TCSM vs. the BBFC at Classic Horror', *Classic Horror*, [Online] (n.d.) Available at: http://classic-horror.com/newsreel/tcsm_vs_the_bbfc#sdendnote2anc [Accessed 23 March 2012].

BAD OMENS

The Texas Chain Saw Massacre begins with a title crawl, the white text that is set against a black background read out to the audience by a solemn narrator (John Larroquette):

> The film you are about to see is an account of the tragedy that befell a group of five youths, in particular Sally Hardesty and her invalid brother, Franklin. It is all the more tragic in that they were young. But, had they lived very, very long lives, they could not have expected nor would they have wished to see as much of the mad and the macabre as they were to see on that day. For them an idyllic summer afternoon drive became a nightmare. The events of that day were to lead to the discovery of one of the most bizarre crimes in the annals of American history. The Texas Chain Saw Massacre.

This narration is perhaps an odd way to begin the film for it tells the audience exactly what is going to happen and to whom. The element of surprise, shock and horror is (potentially) quelled, for the audience now know, within moments of the film starting, some or all of the youths are not going to live to the end of the film. But, perhaps, this is the point: it is not *who* is going to die but *how*. The conclusion of the narration declares the film's title, *The Texas Chain Saw Massacre*. By announcing the title, the content of the narration is given a context and a definition, a quality enhanced by the manner in which the title is spoken by Larroquette: a word, a pause, a word, a pause and so forth. This not only adds a solemn gravitas to each word but also, significantly, breaks the title down into four discreet and powerfully resonant words:

> *The* is the definite article, suggesting that what has been described and what is about to follow is a definitive account of an actual atrocity that happened in Texas. It is, as Rick Worland suggests, *the* massacre, 'the one [that] everybody has heard about' (2007: 211).

Texas firmly locates the described events within a contemporary real-world location. By using the name of a State, the *reality* of the forthcoming account is consolidated and further amplified because it happened in the here and now, in the state of Texas. The explicit reference to Texas carries additional connotations: as already discussed, certain crew members had reservations about the use of it within the title, with Art Director

Robert Burns commenting that :

> Texas already had a bad reputation because of the murder of JFK and *Time* magazine
> did a piece where Texas was spelled using graphics – like the 'A' was a Ku Klux Klan
> hat… So we'd just come out of a terrible reputation when the picture started.
> (Jaworzyn, 2003: 93)

Such a comment points to the historical and stereotypical resonances of the word:
the Battle of the Alamo, JFK's assassination, the Charles Whitman shooting spree at the
University of Texas, alongside notions of small and insular farming communities, rednecks,
racism, homophobia, inbreeding, and a constant, intense heat. All combine to construct
an (actually unfounded) image of a violent, brutal and intolerant populace.

The words *Chain Saw* describe the device by which the described youths will meet
their demise. The mechanical object to which these words refer is one that connotes a
technological interaction within the pastoral of agriculture. Worland suggests that the
chain saw is:

> … a tool commonly used by the rural working class for small chores as well as one
> that can be employed for destruction on a mass industrial scale in logging or the
> slaughterhouse industry to cut up carcasses. (2007: 211)

The connotations of the device become one of a hand-held machine that extends
both the reach and power of its user, temporarily investing them with the 'strength'
to perform the latter destructive acts upon nature. Destructive violence is therefore
implicit in its name, a quality which, in relation to the deaths of the youths, implies
barbaric assault or, at the very least, a severe and violent amputation – at worse
a grotesquely mutilated corpse. Either way, *Chain Saw* implies bloody carnage that
amplifies the final word, *Massacre*.

As defined in the *OED*, a massacre is the 'indiscriminate and brutal slaughter of many
people… [To] deliberately and brutally kill (many people)'. In relation to the narration,
the massacre will be paired down to the five youths, their deaths brutal and without
reason. While the word resonates in relation to the narration and, being the last word
of it, clearly creates both an atmosphere and tension for the audience, the word itself
carries a greater weight at the time of the film's production and release: for both the US

and the global populace the word massacre had become indelibly associated with the events at My Lai in Vietnam (ibid.). Over the course of three hours on 16 March 1968, a platoon of US soldiers from Charlie Company killed between 347 and 400 unarmed civilians, many of whom were women, children, babies and the elderly. As these people were executed, other atrocities were taking place – women were gang raped, others beaten, hit with rifle butts, stabbed with bayonets or tortured. Investigations into the incident initially led to 26 US soldiers being charged but only one, Second Lieutenant William Calley, was convicted. For his part in the massacre, Calley was sentenced to life imprisonment but would only serve three-and-a-half years before being released. The My Lai massacre became public knowledge in 1969, immediately causing global outrage. As a consequence, US domestic opposition to the country's involvement in the Vietnam War increased. As Worland indicates, by using a single powerful word, 'a low-budget horror movie managed to… call up some of the bitterest social and political schisms of the day' (ibid.).

As the last of the narration disappears off the screen, another title appears: *August 18, 1973*. Its brief presence compounds the documentary atmosphere implied by the opening narration by providing specific 'factual' detail to 'the mad and macabre' events that the five unfortunate youths would experience on that 'idyllic summer afternoon'. For Worland, the presence of the date adds a further authenticity as it functions 'as if detailing facts in a crime report' (2007: 212). As a consequence, the first minute of *The Texas Chain Saw Massacre* projects not only a strong sense of doom but of *reality*, of a sense of *authenticity*.[1] The implication of the narration is to establish a trusting relationship with the audience in that what they are about to witness is in fact *real*, a cinematic retelling of an *actual* event. Consequentially, even before the actual film itself has started, a strong sense of horrific anticipation is intimated. But, in sharp contrast to this implied documentary mode, *The Texas Chain Saw Massacre* begins proper as the date fades down to black and a truly mad and macabre montage of sound and image follow.

THE CRIME

The montage begins with a sustained period of darkness, a black screen held for fifteen seconds or more as the audience hears what is taking place within that shadow – the sound of digging, dirt sliding off the shovel, laboured breath and then the sound of wood splintering. A sudden and sharp whining sound and an image briefly appears – a close-up of a camera's flash bulb. There is a brief period of darkness before the flash is triggered once more and the sharp, whining sound is heard over an image of a skeletal hand. The fingers curl inward, fingernails are missing, the rotting flesh seemingly dripping from the bone. Following this pattern of darkness, flash bulb and deathly fragments in an unsteady rhythm, the montage details what appears to be an exhumation: details of the corpse appear, albeit briefly, in the glare of the flash, split-seconds in which hands, the skull, crooked teeth, and rotting clothes are all momentarily seen. For a moment we think this may be a legal exhumation, for the flashes of light indicate a documenting of evidence. But the images begin to appear with increasing rapidity, a fevered succession of grotesque details that now depict not a legal act but an illegal one, the perpetrator of which is feeling an intense excitement: a violation of a corpse is taking place under the cover of darkness, a secret and depraved act which contextualises the opening narration – mad and macabre, the summer turned to a nightmare, the most bizarre crime in the annals of American history.

Accompanying the images is a dual soundtrack: the sound effects continue and aurally describe the ripping of flesh, bones being twisted and possibly snapped, hands – young and supple – rubbed together in some sort of perverse glee or pride. A further series of non-diegetic sounds are heard beneath these narrative sound effects – ambient drones, cymbals rolling and crashing, and dull echoes all merging into one another to create an abstract soundtrack that seemingly 'scrapes' against the imagery and the act of violation they depict. Mumbling beneath these sounds is a further non-diegetic sound, a radio broadcast of a news report that details a number of horrific incidents.

As this layering of sound continues, the montage comes to an end with a low-angle close-up of a corpse's skull, an image made all the more discomforting as it appears against the bleached backdrop of the early morning sky of 18 August 1973. Given its appearance and the state of decay, it is assumed that it is the skull of the exhumed

Evidence of the Hitchhiker's 'grizzly work of art'.

corpse. This image is held for a short period, the camera revelling in the full exposure of what has only just been glimpsed in darkness, detailing the slick purification and the wisps of grey hair that catch in the light breeze. The camera slowly begins to pull back from the corpse, as the sound of the radio broadcast is increased to match the abstract soundtrack:

> Grave robbing in Texas is this hour's top news story. An informant led officers at Marto County sheriff department to a cemetery, just outside the small rural Texas community of Newt early this morning. Officers there discovered what appeared to be a grizzly work of art. The remains of a badly decomposed body, wired to a large monument. A second body was found in the ditch near the perimeter of the cemetery. Subsequent investigation has revealed at least a dozen empty crypts and it's clear more will turn up as the probe continues.

As the events of the montage are verbally recounted and confirmed through this radio broadcast, the camera continues to pull back to reveal 'the grisly work of art': the trousers of the corpse have been cut to allow the body to be 'impaled' upon a stone monument, its leg held open and akimbo to the structure in a sexually provocative manner. Its arms are folded so as to rest upon the apex of the monument, the palms turned upward so that they may hold the severed head of another corpse.

The camera, having fully revealed the horror of the corpses, once again holds the image as the remainder of the radio broadcast continues:

> Deputies report that in some instances only parts of the corpses have been removed. The head, or in some cases the extremities removed, and the remainder of the corpse left intact. Evidence indicates the robberies have occurred over a period of time. Sheriff Rhesus Maldonado refuses to give details in this case and said only that he did have strong evidence linking the crime to elements outside the state. Area residents have reportedly converged on the cemetery claiming the remains of relatives have been removed. No suspects are in custody, as investigations at the scene continue.

The news report offers further clues to the forthcoming narrative in that the perpetrator has not only taken certain parts of the corpses but that these 'robberies' have taken place over an unspecified period of time. Whoever is committing these acts is someone who is clearly psychologically aberrant and enjoys either (or both) the process of exhumation or the laws that it breaks. They are also, potentially, taking the body parts to fulfil either a desire to have a trophy of their transgressions or, perhaps more perversely, are taking the limbs in order to slake a fetishistic desire. Such an assumption is compounded by the 'grisly work of art' for it is a deliberate construction that seeks to humiliate and offend as it is an arrangement that crudely unites sexual provocation with the taboo of exhumation, of sex with death. In this construction and the theft of the body parts, there is a clear disregard for the respect for the dead and for the sanctity of the flesh. As a meaningful construction, the 'grisly work of art' is a foreboding totem, a symbol of what is yet to come for Sally Hardesty and her friends: Law (and therefore Order) is disregarded, as is the flesh; psychological chaos roams at large and unchecked; violations will no doubt occur upon these teenagers and, just as harrowingly, once they are dead their bodies will be subject to dismemberment, totemic reconstruction and possibly sexual humiliations. It would seem that there are no boundaries that will not be crossed, no taboos left unexplored, even after their deaths.

It is worth noting that the news report indicates that the local Sheriff has 'strong evidence linking the crime to elements outside the state'. Given that the crime(s) have taken place in the 'small rural Texas community of Newt', an obvious reading of this dialogue would indicate that the townspeople of Newt have a fear the Outsider, of strangers broaching the borders of their seemingly close-knit community and disturbing not just its living populace but also its dead. As a trope within the horror genre, the Outsider is often a figure who is represented as being one who is opposite to the community they enter into. This is usually a person (or persons) from the City entering into the Wilderness in some form of leisure pursuit. While this is a generic convention across many horror films, it is problematic to suggest that the exhumations and subsequent humiliations are the result of actions undertaken by Sally and her friends. On the contrary, it would seem, at least from the audience's perspective, that the perpetrator of these crimes will be the one wielding the chain saw.

With a loud clash of cymbals, the sequence ends with an abrupt cut to the film's brief titles: the white text is set against an abstract background of red and black, Rorschach blots that seem to vibrate or shift. Curves of darkness are defined by thin lines of red, which suddenly – and out of synch with the chaotic soundtrack – expand and ripple outward. Given the opening montage, these may well be abstract images of fresh meat,[2] slabs of flesh being butchered and bleeding across the table. Again, another loud clash of cymbals marks the end of the sequence, cutting to an image of the sun, a burning bright orange disc against the early morning sky. The cymbals reverberate, a cold and hollow sound that contrasts with the warmth of the Texas sun. This slowly dissolves to the first actual image of the narrative proper: a dead armadillo lies on its back at the roadside; a green camper van, in the background and out of focus, drives past and comes to a stop.

This cross dissolve is perhaps the most blatant suggestion within this lengthy opening sequence: the early morning sun, its circular shape and dusty yellow-orange colour are all equated not with life or renewal but with death. As a precursor, the motif of the sun and other solar bodies – most notably the moon and Saturn – will all, in one way or another, be associated with the fatalities mentioned within the opening narration, particularly in their appearance before the murders and partially because of the deathly symbolic value invested in them by this cross-dissolve.

In many respects this protracted opening sequence of narration, montage and title sequence is a visually and aurally complex construction that marks out bad omens for the five teenagers: their deaths are announced at the very start of the film, bodies are being illegally exhumed and constructed into totemic warnings, stories of death, murder and mutilation are heard through radio broadcasts that are mumbling in the background noise, and the sun rises in a peculiar solar conjunction with a dead animal. All, it would seem, on 18 August 1973, is not well.

SATURN, IN RETROGRADE

As the image of the sun and dead armadillo cross-dissolve, the radio news broadcast continues and recounts further horrors as Kirk helps Franklin to the roadside to urinate: a downtown building has collapsed, killing all of its occupants; the bodies of a young man and four children have been found with their faces 'carved away'; a child has been found by police imprisoned within the attic of their parent's home. While these stories continue to reverberate with the implications of the earlier news broadcasts they also implicate a nation in disarray, in that this narrative of 'the mad and the macabre' is taking place in a world that is equally as unbalanced – buildings are collapsing for no reason and children are either abused or murdered. And they function as further bad omens for Sally and her friends for they tangentially inform the horrors they will soon encounter: their world will collapse around them, some will be imprisoned and others murdered.

Cutting to the inside of the camper van, Pam takes up her astrology book and begins to read out the current state of the zodiac's alignment:

> The condition of retrogradation is contrary or inharmonious to the regular direction of the actual movement in the Zodiac and is, in that respect, evil. Hence, when malefic planets are in retrograde and – Saturn's malefic, OK? – these maleficies are increased… it just means Saturn is a bad influence. It's just a particularly bad influence now because it's in retrograde.

While Pam's recounting of the state of Saturn may seem to be the sort of dialogue reinforces the relationships between the teenagers and consolidate their status as hippies, the astrological conditions Pam relates to her friends actually works to define the movement of the narrative itself, describe the condition of the antagonists (and, by

Saturn's malefic, OK?' - Pam's Astrology book warns the teenagers once more of the dangers that lie ahead of them.

the narrative's end, the surviving protagonist), and to consolidate the meaning ascribed to solar imagery in the opening title sequence.

Pam describes Saturn as being in a retrograde state. In astrological terms, to be in this condition means to be moving backwards in orbit. While the narrative of *The Texas Chain Saw* is perpetually, relentlessly forward moving, the actual *events* following Franklin's murder shift into a retrograde state as they constantly turn back upon themselves and so events are repeated. It would seem that as the narrative progresses, time collapses into an ever-decreasing loop, a sequence of repetitious events from which, for Sally at least, there seems to be no escape.

THE CRIME SCENE

Hearing about the grave robberies on the radio, the teenagers make a detour to the graveyard to establish whether or not a Hardesty grave has been defiled. This brief sequence develops two of the major concerns of the film – its preoccupation with negative portents and the stylistic manner in which the narrative is itself depicted, the qualities of which are combined in the character of an unnamed local drunk.

Pulling into the graveyard, Sally gets out to ask a group of locals who she can talk to about the grave robberies. A mixture of the young and old, these characters fulfil the stereotype of the Texan/rural American – cowboy hats and boots, sunglasses, dungarees and pipes, broad Texan accents. As they discuss whom Sally should talk to, Hooper cuts to a low-angle shot of another member of their group: a drunk lies almost prone inside an abandoned tyre, his drink dribbling down his chin. He laughs at Sally's comments and, with Franklin watching him, slowly slides to the ground and says:

> Things happen hereabouts they don't tell you about… I see things. You see they say it's just an old man talking. You laugh at an old man. There is them that laughs and them that knows better.

As another portent, the drunk's dialogue is obvious but, at a more complex level, his comments indicate a wider understanding of the grave robberies in that they are part of a series of other dubious incidents. These 'things that happen hereabouts' is deliberately ambiguous, but the implication is that not only have these illegal exhumations and humiliations happened before, but they are widely known of in the community, if not openly discussed.

The visual manner in which this dialogue is presented to the audience (and, through the use of point of view shots, to Franklin) is typical of the film's emerging style: while the opening narration suggested a docudrama, Hooper now opts instead for a style which, as Lucy Fife Donaldson (2010) indentifies, 'is characterised by a mixture of extremes'. Instead of presenting the graveyard sequence and the drunk's dialogue in a linear format, Hooper uses long-shots punctuated with short sequences filmed from unusual angles, and makes dialogue function as a type of sound bridge, taking the form of voice-over narration: as Sally is led to her grandfather's grave, Hooper cuts to Franklin wheeling himself forward in the van and looking down. He then cuts to his point of view, in medium close-up, of the drunk, who is prostrate and appears upside down within the frame. He begins the aforementioned dialogue during which Hooper cuts back to Sally – in long-shot – walking towards the grave with the drunk's dialogue continuing over this image. Hooper then cuts back to the drunk who finishes speaking, and then back to Franklin, who wheels himself back inside the van.

In this short sequence, the 'mixture of extremes' is apparent in the combination of shot distance to subject and the sustaining of the drunk's dialogue over the images. One potential reading of this mode lies in the inverted nature of Franklin's point of view, for it indicates a steady disorientation or fragmentation within the narrative as much as it amplifies the negative portents implicated within the dialogue. This is enhanced by the long-shot of Sally, for it is clear by her actions she is speaking to another character but such is the distance between her and the camera that her dialogue cannot be heard nor her facial expressions/reactions seen. Consequently, the sequence suggests a disruption within a linear narrative flow, an incidence of destabilisation that reoccurs and accelerates throughout the film, becoming more and more extreme, achieved by integrating low-angle shots with out-of-focus images and intense close-ups. Such is the extent of this 'mixture of extremes' that the style of the film, in its final stages, gives itself up to the insanity of the narrative and assumes the logic of a nightmare, the soundtrack abandoning conventional dialogue for Sally's constant screaming, the insane babble and unhinged threats of the cannibal family and the almost constant whirr of Leatherface's chain saw.

THE HITCHHIKER

Sustaining this unconventional style, Hooper cuts from the exterior of the cemetery to a long-shot of the van, linking the shift in time and place through a line of Sally's dialogue: spoken as if in voice-over, she reassures Franklin that their grandfather's grave had not been tampered with. Hooper then cuts to the cluttered interior of the van, where the teenagers make trivial conversation that has nothing to do with the cemetery or Franklin's concerns. As they talk they are distracted by a foul smell; looking out of the van's windows Franklin tells the group they are passing the old slaughterhouse, the place where 'Grandpa used to sell his cattle' and continues by describing what took place inside:

> They bash them over the head with a big sledgehammer. It usually wouldn't kill them on the first lick then they would start squealing and freaking out and everything and then they would have to come up to them and bash them two or three times and then sometimes that wouldn't kill 'em. I mean they would skin 'em sometimes even before they were even dead.

The Hitchhiker - a slaughter man, psychopath, cannibal.

While Franklin's dialogue disgusts both his friends[3] and the audience both in its graphic nature and his enthusiastic recounting of it, Franklin's dialogue is really just another bad omen, a portent that is no different to the opening narration insofar as it functions to prepare the audience for what is going to happen to Kirk (and, much later, Sally) in particular.

As Franklin speaks, Hooper cuts back to an exterior shot of the slaughterhouse, Franklin's description continuing as a voice-over to these images: cattle are bunched tightly together in a metal pen, braying as they shuffle around each other. The camera lingers on a medium close-up of one cow in particular. The animal hangs its head between the bars, eyes rolled up to the whites, tongue lolling and foaming at the mouth. It is a disturbing face of a docile creature's impending death, made all the more so as the frame 'decapitates' the animal in signification of its impending demise. This image and the dialogue that 'narrates' it can only mean one thing for Kirk, his girlfriend and their friends – they too are cattle heading for the slaughter. Compounding this is the subsequent wide-angle shot that closes this sequence: the camper van drives past the camera and continues on down the road. As the camera follows its path, it takes in the numerous telegraph poles that line the road – each is a wooden upright with a single bar running

Cattle to the slaughter…

across it and so creates an avenue of crosses, a line of grave markers through which the teenagers drive towards the fateful transition from idyllic summer afternoon to nightmare. The implication of the layering of dialogue and image in this sequence is the first clear suggestion that, in the internal (insane) logic of *The Texas Chain Saw Massacre*, purpose-bred cattle have been replaced by innocent passers-by. In an oblique manner, Hooper presents the audience with its first cryptic signifier of the antagonists' cannibalistic consumption.

As the group continue their drive, they see a hitchhiker up ahead and, because of the intense heat, decide to pick him up, despite Pam and Franklin airing their concerns. Pulling over, they slide open the doors and let him in: wearing slack, flared jeans, a loose, green T-shirt and with long, greasy hair, the young man appears to be about their age and, given his appearance, also a hippy. He has a birthmark that runs the length of his face, is carrying an animal-skin bag and has a Polaroid camera hanging from his neck. Once inside the van, the teenagers and audience meet the first real monster of *The Texas Chain Saw Massacre*, a notion clearly visually articulated by the fact that 'Hitchhiker' sits at one end of the van as the teenagers gather together at the opposite end. Facing each other, Franklin verbalises the tension by commenting to his friends that 'I think we just picked up Dracula'. The teenagers ask Hitchhiker questions about where he's from and where he's going, the answers to which are sometimes enthusiastically given or carefully avoided, their concerns compounded by his nervous and jittery nature. As they talk, it becomes apparent that both he and his family worked in the slaughterhouse they have only just passed, a fact he evidences through Polaroids of animal carcasses. As the teenagers look at these washed-out images of cattle carcasses, Hitchhiker tells them that his 'family's always been in meat', that the introduction of the airgun to kill the cattle put people 'out of jobs' and declares that 'I was the killer'. While Hitchhiker's dialogue functions as a means by which to introduce him to both the protagonist and the audience, his answers also start to subtly reveal other significations of cannibalism and the reason for such an act.

At the centre of this is Hitchhiker's statement that the shift from manual labour to industrialisation in the slaughterhouse has led to him and his family's unemployment. Within the context of the narrative, the advent of new technological means to slaughter has meant a more humane death for the cattle but has rendered those previously employed as redundant. Without employment in the slaughter trade, Hitchhiker and (it is presumed) his family have been severed from both normal society and their ancestry. The former is somewhat lamented by Hitchhiker (who perceives the industrialisation of slaughter not only as a means by which jobs are lost but also the loss of a valuable set of skills) while the latter has, in some way, caused the steady decline into primitivism/ cannibalism. Thus, Hitchhiker's comment that 'My family has always been in meat' carries a double meaning in that the young man's ancestry is in slaughter work but, without employment, the family have simply carried this tradition in private. Read this way, the subsequent attacks upon Sally's friends function as a perverse political act whereby the have-nots 'eat the rich', the Rural violently assaults the Urban: it is first an act of revenge for the loss of employment, a context in which, Christopher Sharrett suggests, the act cannibalism becomes the 'ultimate revenge on a foe or his progeny by devouring his strength and redressing a long-term historical debt' (1996: 265) and, perversely, as a means by which a proud ancestry can be maintained and traditional methods still practised.

In his seminal *An Introduction to the American Horror Film* (1979), Robin Wood notes that there is consequently a certain ambivalence in the audience's response to the cannibal family. This is primarily due to the fact that the three brothers are a family and are therefore subject to the various tensions all families are subject to – argument, struggles for authority, rivalries and resentments. Wood indicates that the ambivalent feeling is amplified by the fact that the men are victims themselves, stating that 'there is the sense that *they* are victims too – of the slaughterhouse environment, of capitalism' (1979: 190). The implication is that the brothers themselves are not directly responsible for their actions but have been, in some way, reduced to these violent and grotesque acts as the capitalist society has rejected them. As efficient as these men may be at slaughter, a machine can do it even quicker and requires only maintenance, not financial reward. Struggling to survive in a rural environment, the men have responded to their rejection through violent retribution, the cost of which is not only the lives of those murdered but also their own sanity.

The conversation soon dwindles and the tension between the young adults increases until Hitchhiker performs a series of increasingly bizarre rituals. First, he takes a penknife from Franklin and cuts open his own palm. He then offers Kirk his own knife – a cut-throat razor concealed within his sock – and indicates that he too should cut himself. When he refuses, Hitchhiker then takes Franklin's photograph. When he asks for money for the image, the group refuse. Hitchhiker then places the photograph on a piece of tin foil, pours gunpowder on it and then ignites it. As the others scream and shout, he quickly extinguishes it and puts the charred remains into his animal-fur pouch. Disturbed by his actions, Jerry pulls the van over and the group push Hitchhiker out. As the van pulls away, he smears his bloody palm across the vehicle and, in a childish insult, sticks out his tongue and spits at the moving vehicle.

To calm the tension in the van, Jerry asks Pam to read out Franklin's horoscope:

Travel in the country, long-range plans and upsetting persons around you could make this a disturbing and unpredictable day. The events in the world are not doing much either to cheer one up.

Pam then reads out Sally's prediction:

Oh no… Capricorn is ruled by Saturn. There are moments when we cannot believe that what is happening is really true. Pinch yourself and you may find out that it is.

If the suggestive nature of these horoscopes were not enough, Hooper reinforces their implication by cutting from this line of dialogue to an exterior shot of a petrol station: the forecourt attendant looks up at the sky and, cutting to his point of view, the perfect circle of the pale yellow sun against a pale blue sky, is placed centrally in the frame, clouds drifting past. It would seem that, for all the mockery ('Hey man, do you believe all that stuff your old lady's hawking me?' says Jerry) of Pam's belief in astrology, astral and perhaps supernatural forces seemingly are at work, steadily orchestrating events that will lead the five teenagers into danger and, for most, to their deaths.

A FURTHER WARNING

While the two girls go to the petrol station restroom and get a Coke, the three boys stay in the van and talk to the petrol station owner. Franklin asks if he knows the location of his grandparent's house and describes it to him, to which he replies that he may have seen such a house, but:

> You boys don't wanna go messing around an old house. Those things is dangerous. You're liable to get hurt… You don't wanna go fooling around other folks' property. Some folks don't like it and they don't mind showing you.

The girls get back into the camper van and the boys decide to ignore the advice they have just been given: eating the barbecue they have purchased from the petrol station, they drive off to find the ancestral home of the Hardesty family.

ENDNOTES

1. It is worth noting that when the Secretary of the Board for the BBFC, Stephen Murphy, first watched the film, he stated in a memo that the film 'appeared to be a fictionalised documentary'.

2. These images are, in fact, recordings of solar flares: when discussing the later stages of editing the film, Sallye Richardson comments that Hooper and herself did not feel the beginning worked, 'so we shot the opening scene with the corpse statue of Warren's, bought the sunspot footage from NASA in Houston and added the crawl' (Jaworzyn, 2003: 75).

3. The idea that Pam is a somewhat stereotypical hippy is reinforced by her response to Franklin's description: 'People shouldn't kill animals for food' implying that she is either a vegetarian or vegan.

REFERENCES

Donaldson, L. F., 2010. Access and Excess in *The Texas Chain Saw Massacre. Movie*, [Online]. (1). Available at: http://www2.warwick.ac.uk/fac/arts/film/movie/pastissues/ [Accessed 23 March 2012].

Jaworzyn, S., 2003. *The Texas Chain Saw Massacre Companion*. London: Titan Books.

Marriott, J. & Newman, K. eds., 2006. *Horror: The Definitive Guide to the Cinema of Fear*, London: Andre Deutsch Limited.

Worland, R., 2007. *The Horror Film: An Introduction*. Oxford: Blackwell Publishing.

THE CHARNEL HOUSE

The ancestral home, the site of memories and totems.

In their book *The Gothic* (2004) David Punter and Glennis Byron open their Introduction by stating that the Gothic is 'a notoriously difficult field to define' (xvii) primarily because of the extensive critical engagements with its long and complex history. Originating in the late eighteenth century, the genre has steadily evolved by continually building upon a range of recurrent motifs, which in turn have been 'borrowed' and integrated into other genres and a broad range of media. This constant shift has made defining the Gothic significantly problematic. As Punter and Byron identify, definitions ultimately become a reduction to personal critical judgement, with academics presenting *their* definition of the Gothic at the beginning of their critical texts. This has led to an intriguing and potentially diverse range of possible definitions for the genre but, despite this, there remains an 'extraordinary persistence of certain motifs' across the works claimed to be 'Gothic' and it is with these motifs that Punter and Byron structure their book: theirs is not an attempt 'to define the Gothic but rather to present some of its parameters and to describe some of the terrain that lies within those parameters' (xx). These parameters include the Haunted Castle, the Monster and Persecution and Paranoia.[1] Unsurprisingly, these motifs are intrinsic to interpreting *The Texas Chain Saw Massacre*, for they appear either full-blown or in subverted form throughout the text.[2] Such is the intensity – both emotionally and contextually – of these occurrences that it is possible to cite *Chain Saw* within the Gothic genre.

THE HAUNTED CASTLE(S)

The group of teenagers leave the petrol station and drive to the Hardesty house: first seen in long-shot, the house itself is obscured[3] by trees and the creepers that have grown over the majority of its façade. Accompanying the image is a foreboding soundtrack – a low *rumble* that that is layered with gusts of wind and an eerie, low echo which shifts in pitch. Such a mix of sounds intimates the *emptiness* of the house, its very *hollowness*, the darkness of its shadows and recesses. When coupled with the long-shot, this makes clear reference to the numerous haunted houses that have populated the horror genre since its inception. Leaving Franklin outside to look at the smear of blood left by Hitchhiker on the side of the van, the others go inside, the camera following them to reveal the interior to be in a state of ruin: even though its windows are broken and the sun high, the rooms and long corridors are filled with deep shadow and a soft, blue tint, the wallpaper faded and peeling, the stairwell and floorboards rotten. As a space of ancestry for Sally and Franklin and given its state of decay, the Hardesty house makes clear correlations with Punter and Byron's descriptor of the haunted castle: identifying its origins in the *first* Gothic novel – Horace Walpole's *The Castle of Otranto* (1764) – Punter and Byron describe these locations as a space of feudal magnificence that is contrasted with its collapsing and poorly lit interior. With their crumbling walls and labyrinthine, darkly lit corridors that lead to lower levels, cellars and dungeons, these haunted castles are a space of gloom and murk, deep shadow and pools of light. All are resonant of memory and imprisonment, oppression and repression, to ultimately become 'a site of secrets' (2004: 261).

For Sally, this is not a house of horror but one of fond memories. She wanders through the corridors and rooms with a childish fascination, running her fingers through the decay as she recounts to Jerry and Pam the times spent with her grandparents. They pause in the room that Sally describes as the nursery, explaining it was the space in which she and Franklin slept. She places her hand on the peeling wallpaper and comments on the faded depictions of wild animals:

These animals would to put me to sleep when I was a little girl. Look at the zebra. I
had this fascination for the zebras...

For Sally, the house, or at least what remains of it, is a container of the past, a physical
space permanently locked in an era to which she can only return to through her
memories. As such, Sally's response to the structure evidences a further quality of
Punter and Byron's haunted castle in that these architectures are sites in which history is
'compressed into a single image' (2004: 259). Although the physical structure may be in
a state of collapse, the resonance of event and experience remain firmly located in that
space and, in terms of the Gothic at least, allow for one of its most significant tropes to
be made manifest – the return of the past into the present. Such an occurrence *usually*
takes the form of a spectre, a ghost that wanders those dim corridors in order to either
warn the protagonist of impending danger or to seek their help to release them from
limbo. But for Sally, her grandparents' home is not haunted. There are no ghosts here,
only their memory.

In contrast to Sally's response, and despite his ancestral connection to the building,
Franklin finds the house to be impregnable and a foreshadowing of horrors to come.
Franklin attempts to enter the building but struggles to negotiate the debris with his
wheelchair. He eventually gets to the remains of the porch and pulls himself up and into
the gloom. Resting for a moment, he listens to Jerry's muted voice and Sally's laughter.
As he pushes himself through the doorway, he mutters insults about his sister and her
friends, childishly sticking out his tongue and spitting. Alone, he wheels himself through
the corridors and turns to leave but, as he does so, he enters another room that has
a bizarre tableaux resting upon the splintered floorboards: although Hoper affords
the construction a sustained close-up, it is difficult to tell exactly which this macabre
arrangement is. Resting on what appears to be a filthy pillow is either the desiccated
remains of a bird or an animal, its wings or limbs spread wide and the exposed bones
laced with feathers. Franklin looks upon it in horror, a further ritualistic occurrence
that, for him, tallies with Hitchhiker's equally bizarre ritual of burning his photograph.
He calls out for Sally and, in doing so, looks up to ceiling. Attached to the door-frame
directly above him is an animal bone totem – various bones and feathers pierced and
threaded onto fraying string. It slowly rotates in the wind, a contemporary and perverse
reworking of Damocles Sword, hanging by its thread in possible judgement.

The objects that Franklin finds[4] function primarily to sustain the film's initial and explicit preoccupation with littering the teenagers' path with portents of doom. These arrangements of feather, bone and rotting flesh are all precursors not to their deaths but to the second haunted house that most of this small group will enter. As 'mad and macabre' arrangements, they clearly frighten Franklin who has, since the discovery of the bloody smear on the side of the van, become increasing concerned that Hitchhiker is pursuing them with the intent to kill him. As 'grisly works of art', it is more than likely that Franklin is correct in his supposition that these objects were gathered and arranged by Hitchhiker. These evidences of insanity reconfigure the Hardesty house: no longer the site of nostalgia (for Sally, at least), the decaying house has become the site of disturbing ritual, a secret space in which arcane acts are performed. The manner in which the desiccated corpse is presented – carefully laid out and the feathers seemingly arranged in a pattern – suggest some sort of totemic sacrifice and deathly worship.

From the perspective of anthropology and ethnology, a totem is an object that is, more often than not, an animal or plant that functions as the symbol of a clan, tribe or family and, for that social group, contains ritualistic associations. Considered in this way, the two articles Franklin discovers can be considered to be emblematic of Hitchhiker and his family, a quality made clear when Pam enters their actual home – for it is, as will be seen, a site of feather and bone. By placing these emblems in the Hardesty ancestral home, these arrangements function as an encroachment into and appropriation of the Hardesty home, a means by which Hitchhiker's family demonstrate their trespass into that property and mark it as their own. In ritualistic terms, the objects reference arcane spells that have, in conjunction with the cosmic disarray caused by Saturn's maleficies, somehow exerted their powers upon the teenagers and drawn them to this space.

Disturbed by what he has found, Franklin tries to leave the building but is stopped by Kirk and Pam who ask him about the swimming hole that is on the property. He gives them directions and watches them leave. Unable to easily move around or get Sally's attention, Franklin sits in the shadow and waits, director Hooper cutting from the interior darkness of the house to the immense bright of its exterior as Kirk and Pam follow the route described by Franklin. The land adjoining the Hardesty house is transformed by the heat into a romantic rural idyll, a place of fertile growth, lush corn and ripe green grass, deep blue skies. The manner in which their walk is shot and

The front of Leatherface's home - the facade of respectability.

the purpose of their journey implies that a romantic or sexual interlude between the teenagers is about to occur. The couple talk, run and laugh, their conversation and movement shot through the golden haze of the mid-day sun. But instead of finding the swimming hole and enjoying an intimate moment, the couple come upon another house.[5]

Like the Hardesty house, this new home is seen by the teenagers and the audience through lush green trees, its white clapboard apex appearing to bleach out in the sun. On the soundtrack is the sound of a generator. Realising that the generator is petrol powered, Kirk decides to approach the occupants of the house and ask if he can buy some fuel in order to enable the group to get back to the petrol station. Pam doesn't seem so sure but follows Kirk into the property. Entering through the backyard, Kirk and Pam walk through parched grounds of rural decay: the ground is dirt and weed from which bare trees grow. Their branches are adorned with metal cups and jugs, each suspended by a string tied to the handle. Nearby, a ripped tarpaulin is stretched across the space between two trees and lashed tight to form some sort of shelter. The cups and jugs clank together in the wind. In among these rusting objects is a pocket watch. Shown in close-up, it has had a nail driven through its centre and a faded pink ribbon tied to the pointed end. It slowly rotates in the wind like the feather and bone charm.

As a further totemic symbol, the watch is, as Mark Bould states, a 'puzzling image' (2003: 99): having been penetrated by the nail, the pocket watch in *Chain Saw* is rendered inoperable and so functions as a symbolic attempt to stop time. Bould suggests the watch signifies 'the extent to which the slaughterhouse family are determined to halt the passage of time, to resist history' (ibid: 108). While the watch totem clearly (and quite literally) stops time it is not necessarily evocative of resisting history. Given the earlier discussion of Hitchhiker's comments about the shift to industrialisation, it would seem that instead of resisting history, his family want to resist progress. Such an interpretation compounds the previous readings whereby Hitchhiker and family are fixated upon the past: by symbolically stopping time Hitchhiker and his family can remain in the past and so sustain their ancestral traditions and heritage.

Kirk and Pam continue to walk towards the property, with Kirk pausing at a row of dilapidated sheds. They have rusted down to the bare bones of their basic structure. The corrugated metal roof and walls have been replaced by a large section of camouflage netting. Kirk peers in between the gaps and calls Pam over to look inside too – beneath the netting stands an array of rusting cars. Some look like farm vehicles, while others appear to be for domestic use. Kirk mutters something about it being crazy but neither he nor Pam quite realise what the presence and neglected state of these seemingly abandoned cars might mean. As they both round the corner of the house, the sound of the generator fades and is replaced by birdsong. Looking at the front of the house, the couple notice a stark difference in appearance – while the back is a mass of rust, decay and rot, the front is a near-perfect image of the rural retreat. Clean white clapboard, a well-kept porch, vivid green trees which dapple the sunlight on a swing adjacent to the building. The house looks, to all intense and purpose, respectable, even welcoming. As Pam sits down on the porch steps, Kirk politely knocks on the door and calls out his greeting. He turns to Pam and, as he does so, kicks something on the floor. Picking it up, he realises it's a human tooth which he places into Pam's hand. She screams and, demanding that they leave, walks off to sit on the swing. Laughing to himself, Kirk knocks on the door once more and it slowly opens. Ignoring the advice given to him by the petrol station owner, Kirk crosses the threshold uninvited, calling out as he does so.

The interior of this home shares a similarity with the Hardesty house in that it too is shrouded in shadow. Kirk ventures into the hallway and looks around: a dark wooden

staircase, the walls adorned with either peeling wallpaper or cattle skins. At the far end
is a doorway with a ramp broaching the threshold between the two spaces. In the
half-light Kirk can make out a vivid, blood-red wall which is decorated with many stuffed
animal heads, presumably trophies of the many kills the occupant has made. Thinking he
is alone, Kirk turns to leave but as he does so he hears what sounds like a pig squealing.
Curious, he returns and walks up the ramp, only to slip. As he gets up he is confronted
by a large figure filling the frame of the doorway who, without hesitation, batters him
over the head with a lump hammer.

THE MONSTER

Leatherface - murderer, psychopath, cannibal.

The figure of the monster is perhaps both the Gothic's and horror's central image. As
either a physical or supernatural being, they are the source of the tension, threat and
violence of the narrative. Their actions – be they murderous or simply the relentless
pursuit of the protagonist – drive the narrative forward towards its deathly end, a
culmination in which, for the most part, the monster is vanquished in graphic and, at
times, euphoric terms. From a more complex perspective, the monster performs what
Punter and Byron define as 'cultural work' by stating that:

> Through difference, whether in appearance or behaviour, monsters function to define
> and construct the politics of the 'normal'. Located at the margins of culture, they
> police the boundaries of the human, pointing to those lines that must not be crossed.
> (2004: 263)

The first appearance of *Chain Saw*'s monster, Leatherface, is as sudden and as brutal as
his first action, the murder of Kirk. He is seen from the perspective of his victim's eyes,
for as the audience watch, a shape appears above the teenager, Hooper cuts to Kirk's
point of view as he gets up: the camera slowly pans upward, taking in the massive bulk
of this man, lingering on the crumpled pink shirt and the dark splashes on the apron he
wears. As the camera rises, so too does the lump hammer, distracting both Kirk and the
viewer and allowing only the briefest glimpse of his face and neck. A dark blue patterned
tie is tightly drawn to the neck and hangs neatly over the apron, a sharp contrast to the
face, which appears to be deformed, with a yellow tint and creased in the wrong places.
The hammer comes down and Hooper cuts back to the long-shot of the hall. Kirk falls,
the murderer shrieks, hits the boy once more and throws the body into the room,
slamming the metal door shut.

In this brief scene, traces of Punter and Byron's descriptor are evident. Leatherface's
appearance and behaviour both contradict the 'normality' that the teenagers represent
through the bizarre juxtaposition of the shirt and tie with the bloody apron and the
lump hammer, coupled with the seemingly disfigured face. The clothes connote business,
while the apron, in the context of the film, clearly connotes slaughter. The wearing
of one over the other suggests a uniform, a costume that evokes the mundanity of
work which, in this case, is murder. The brutality of Kirk's death is not just the speed by
which it happens and the actual appearance of Leatherface but the business-like nature
of the murder – there is no dialogue, no discussion, just a single hammer blow that
effectively does the job, with a second for luck. As Kirk's body convulses on the wooden
ramp, Leatherface hits him once more. Quickly and efficiently, he has slaughtered this
'cattle', throwing it to one side in order for it to be processed and butchered. While
this murderous behaviour is hardly 'normal' and so marks out a line that should not be
crossed, the locating of Leatherface at the very margins of culture is not yet that explicit.
His house seems to be close to a main road and therefore not isolated. Its outward
appearance is one of cleanliness and respectability, while what we have seen of its

interior, albeit decorated with cattle skins and animal heads, is not disturbingly unusual. For Leatherface to fully emerge as Punter and Byron's monster, Pam and Jerry both need to trespass deeper into his house.

Outside, Pam sits on the swing waiting for Kirk. She calls out his name and then gets up and walks to the porch, the camera following behind her. With the camera positioned in this way, Hooper reinforces the disturbing contrast between interior and exterior, for as the camera tracks Pam's movements, the rural idyll is made apparent through the clear blue sky, the soft white clouds, the vivid green trees and the bright sunshine giving the house a warm and welcoming glow. There is nothing for Pam to fear here, yet the homely image is undercut for the audience not only because of Kirk's murder (and surely that fate is going to befall Pam if she too explores further) but precisely because the camera is *behind* her. In this position, the details of Pam's costume is revealed – her blouse is cut and shaped at the back to reveal the majority of her back, while her red shorts are cut tight to her thighs and groin. This is a sexualised image that presents Pam as a slender and desirable young woman, yet the narrative has little preoccupation with sexual union or gratification. Instead, it is one which is intensely preoccupied with *flesh*, with the meat upon the bones. And this is why this image is so harrowing, for it depicts Pam as available meat. The exposure of her back is provocative not in conventional sexual terms but in the anticipation of violence upon it – Hooper knows what is coming and, cruelly, constructs his frame to foreground Pam's back, which will shortly be penetrated and broken.

Pam crosses the threshold, entering into the gloom as she searches for Kirk. She walks towards the red room of animal heads but, distracted by the muffled cawing of a chicken, turns before entering. There is no door, just a heavy grey curtain, slightly parted. She steps forward, opening the curtains as she does so, but trips on a metal bucket[6] and falls to the floor.

THE SLAUGHTERHOUSE

The room she has fallen into is that of the charnel house. Just as Leatherface was introduced through Kirk's point of view, so too this room is revealed through Pam's gaze. She raises her head from the floor in close-up, Hooper quickly cutting to what she sees: the bare, polished floorboards are covered in a thick layer of feathers and bones. There are lots of teeth, both human and animal, and a recognisably human jawbone lies among it all, the feathers drifting against it. Pam looks up and sees a chicken crammed into a small bird-cage and then across to the furniture. In an inspired, if cruel, visual joke, the chair legs have leg bones wired to them, the arm rests have arm bones attached, the headboard of the settee adorned with skulls. She looks up again and sees mobiles of bone and feather lazily rotating in the draughts. The skeletal remains of a hand hangs in among them, as does an empty turtle shell and a human skull, its mouth penetrated by a cattle horn. Pam tries to stand, slips and staggers, her terror articulated through a rapid montage of details of the room's grotesque décor – piles of bones and skulls in the log basket, the mantelpiece decorated with skulls, rusting tools smeared with congealing blood, more bones, more skulls, a forearm held in stasis by an apparent taxidermy, a light bulb rammed into its upturned palm. Pam manages to get out of the room in an attempt to escape but is caught by Leatherface.

Of all the associations and readings this room evokes, the most pertinent are those connoted by the adornments upon the seating and the severed limb transformed into a lighting fixture. In these horrific moments the crimes of 'The Plainfield Ghoul', Ed Gein, are made evident.

ED GEIN

On 16 November 1957, Bernice Worden, a hardware store owner in Plainfield, Texas went missing. Worden's son told police that Gein had been in the store on the previous evening, purchasing a gallon of anti-freeze, which he said he would collect the following morning. Following this lead, investigators gained entry into Gein's farmhouse and associated property, quickly finding Worden's body in one of the sheds. Having shot her with a .22 calibre rifle, Gein had performed a series of postmortem mutilations upon her corpse: he first decapitated her, then hung the body upside down and proceeded to dress out her body as one would a deer. Compounding this discovery were the contents of Gein's farmhouse, where police found, among other body parts, the severed heads of Mary Hogan (a tavern worker who had been missing since 1954) and Bernice

Worden alongside ten other female heads (all of which had had their cranium sawn off), nine masks of human skin, chair seats and wastepaper baskets made from human skin, a pair of human lips hanging from a string, and a variety of internal organs stored within the refrigerator. Under questioning, Gein told the investigating officers that between 1947 and 1952 he had made repeated visits to three local graveyards, each time with the intention of exhuming the recently buried. Gein claimed that when he was doing this he was in a 'daze-like' state and that, more often than not, he would emerge from this condition. In such circumstances, he would return the grave to good order and return home without taking anything. On those occasions when he remained in the 'daze-like' state, he would exhume the bodies of middle-aged women, particularly those he felt bore some resemblance to his deceased mother. Once back at the farm, Gein would then tan the skins in order to use it as the raw material for the 'woman suit' he was attempting to construct. During his interview, Gein confessed to robbing nine graves, eventually leading investigators to them. Two were subsequently exhumed and were found to be empty, corroborating Gein's confession.

During the many police interviews that took place with Gein and those surrounding his crimes, it became obvious that this was a man who was engaged in a complex and frustrating struggle to establish and release his sexual identity. Gein grew up with his brother, Henry, and mother, Augusta. A deeply religious woman, Augusta would berate and belittle her sons and repeatedly warn them of the dangers and sins of women. While Henry would, on occasion, question his mother, Ed accepted her word and became even more devoted to her. Henry would later die in bushfire (although it is suspected that Gein murdered him) and then, when his mother died, Gein was left alone. Riddled with a singular perspective of women from the repressive regime instilled by his mother, Gein's oedipal complex flourished into murder and mutilation.

Five days after the discoveries at the farmstead, Gein was arraigned on one count of first-degree murder. He entered a plea of not guilty by reason of insanity and was subsequently found mentally incompetent and therefore unable to stand trial. Gein would spend the rest of his life in state mental institutions, dying of respiratory and heart failure as a result of cancer on 26 July 1984.

As stated in chapter 1, Ed Gein was not a direct influence upon Hooper and Henkel when they wrote the original screenplay; but Hooper has stated that he was, when young, aware of Gein's crimes, if not of the actual man himself:

> My relatives who lived in a town close to Ed Gein told me these terrible stories, these tales of human skin lampshades and furniture. I grew up with that like a horror story you tell around a camp-fire. I didn't even know about Ed Gein, I just knew about something that happened that was horrendous. But the image really stuck (Quotes from Tobe Hooper, n.d.).

The similarities between Gein's crimes and *Chain Saw*'s room of feather and bone are hard to ignore, as is the correlation with Leatherface's masks of female faces: as will be discussed later, there is an obvious lack of parental figures in the film, particularly a mother. With Leatherface constructing masks of women's skins and then wearing them, as Gein intended to with his women suit, it is possible to suggest that Leatherface was obsessed, in an oedipal sense, with his mother to such an extent that when she died he could not let go of her and so, through the female face masks he 'became' her. In contrast to this there is the possibility that he was, in some way, sexually repressed by his mother. Upon her death, Leatherface was freed from this condition and gave full vent to his true sexual identity – he desires not to be a strong, muscular man but a female, a woman who in some way represents the image of his mother. In its own crude way, the masks of female faces hides Leatherface's masculine face and *make* him female.

THE ROOM OF FEATHER AND BONE

In their descriptor of the haunted castle, Punter and Byron note that a contradiction exists within its gloomy walls:

> It is also, paradoxically, a site of domesticity, where ordinary life carries on… It can be a place of womb-like security, a refugee from the complex exigencies of the outer world; it can also – at the same time and according to a difference of perception – be a place of incarceration, a place where heroines and others can be locked away from the fickle memory of 'ordinary life'. (2004: 261–62)

This room of feather and bone is perhaps not fully the paradox that Punter and Byron identify but more a chilling parody of the domestic. In this room, in its decoration, the domestic is evident but made perverse by the insane logic of Leatherface and his family. The detritus of their slaughter has been transformed into a sickening decoration, a literal chamber of horrors that is a clear reflection of their transgression from 'normal' to 'abnormal'. In this shift, object and ornament are reconfigured through the grafting of bone and skin, an addition which retains their 'normal' domestic purpose (the seating, the lamp stand, the mantelpiece) to the extent that the domestic, albeit perverted, remains clearly in evidence.

The scattered bones signify murder and possible cannibalism, their reuse as grotesque ornament and decoration, shedding new light on the vehicles that Kirk and Pam found as they broached the boundaries of the property, in that Leatherface and his family:

> ... hoard everything, from the cars of previous victims (their source of gasoline?) to the inedible remains of animals, birds and humans, which, as well as meeting material needs, provide a medium for cultural expression. (Bould, 2003: 108)

In this 'cultural expression' Leatherface and his family have constructed an interior that is solely (and perhaps even ironically) preoccupied with the bodily interior. Having eaten the flesh, what remains of those captured, tortured and murdered are tangible evidences of such acts. It would seem that it is not enough to just consume their flesh. Objects and artefacts need to be constructed from their remains to function as emblems, totems or trophies of their ingestions. Of all the symbols that are within this room the most disturbing is the human skull pierced with a cattle horn: in its physical construction this totem connects with the nailed watch hanging outside the property. As that symbol connoted the desire to stop time, this skull symbol is clearly one of 'stopping life'. While this may seem obvious, the physical penetration of the skull evokes a desire to subject the victim to humiliations and psychological trauma, with Bould suggesting that the construction connotes a violent, deathly oral rape (ibid.) – although, as discussed elsewhere, there is otherwise little evidence of a sexual motive behind the killings. The trophies, then, may become symbols not just of the kill or ingestion but come to, in certain cases, symbolise how such murder took place: a record, as it were, of the atrocities inflicted.

THE KITCHEN

In his capture of Pam, Leatherface is fully revealed. She manages to get outside the front door but he grabs hold of her as she crosses the porch. Drawn out of the gloom by his pursuit, he enters daylight and the full horror of his bulk and face are seen. The dark stains upon his apron are clearly splatters of congealed blood, his jeans are filthy, his work boots worn. But it is his sheer bulk and the appearance of his face that horrifies: he is large man, who briefly struggles to get through the door frame.[7] With the sleeves of his pink shirt rolled up, his thick, muscular arms are revealed. They wrap around Pam, lifting her and engulfing her thin frame. She seems to *disappear* into this man, to be consumed not orally but just by his sheer physicality. As she attempts to free herself from his grip, the man's face is clearly seen. The pale yellow skin is loose and creased, dark lines running haphazardly across the surface, revealing that this man wears a mask of human skin.

Pam, hung on a metal hook, is forced to watch the literal butchering of her boyfriend, Kirk.

Within the horror subgenre of the 'slasher' film, the mask is a significant motif, with three of its most universally famous icons wearing such an item: Jason Voorhees from the *Friday the 13th* series wears a battered hockey mask; Michael Myers from the *Halloween* films wears a featureless white mask; while Leatherface wears his mask of skin. Concealment is pertinent to these killers, for the donning of the mask becomes an act of disguise. By wearing a mask, each of the aforementioned characters hides their identity and, by doing so, *becomes* another person. For Jason and Michael this identity is a blank surface, a mask that reduces 'their' facial features to just eyes, nose and mouth. They are anonymous. In contrast, Leatherface's mask is an ironic anonymity, for it is a construction of identities: peeling the facial features from the skulls of his victims, he has carefully tanned and preserved these sections in order for them to be stitched, person by person, section by section, into a patchwork of identities. In doing this and by wearing this mask of others, Leatherface *becomes* them. This reading is supported by his appearance throughout the film, as he wears three different masks during the course of the narrative, each one reflecting who he wants to be in each of the situations in which he finds himself. As Kim Henkel states, 'Leatherface is one of those characters who is what he wears – his character changes according to the face he puts on' (Jaworzyn, 2003: 43). Gunnar Hansen expands upon this by commenting that:

> The whole idea of [Leatherface] was that the mask reflected who he was now – my feeling was that under the mask there was nothing – if you take the mask away there's no face there. That's how I tried to play him, and I think that's why he's such a horrifying character. So the mask defines who he was… So the three masks were the Killer mask, the Old Lady mask and the Pretty Woman – and the Pretty Woman was because we had company and he was getting all dressed up for dinner, so he put on a pretty face. But that was the idea: the masks express what's going on in his mind, in his little pea brain… (2003: 43–45)

While these constructed masks allow Leatherface to become someone else through concealment, they also function as a violent expression of his psychology. Famed horror author and director Clive Barker has commented that:

> … the mask is, of course, both a means of concealment and one of confession. It covers the human and reveals the *in*human. The man disappears, and a creature of mythic proportions replaces him. (Bradley, 2004: 8)

By wearing the masks, Leatherface conceals his exterior but reveals his insane interior, for they speak not of identity but of Barker's idea of confession: they articulate the process of flaying and of piecing together parts to make a 'new' identity which, in turn, speaks of a fractured psychology. By expressing this, the mask transforms to ironically reveal the reality of Leatherface – the physical man does indeed disappear and is replaced by the horror of his insanity.

Leatherface carries Pam into the red room of animal heads and into the kitchen to perform the film's most notorious scene: the implement of the young girl upon a meat hook. A high-angle shot looks down upon the kitchen, taking in its mess of bloody surfaces, the meat hook hanging, out of focus, from the top left-hand corner of the frame. Leatherface enters with Pam over his shoulder. It is another cruel moment, the exposure of her back not only recalling the exposure and fragility of Pam's body from the earlier scene in which she approached the house but also of what is about to come. Time seems a little protracted as she is carried towards the hook, extending the tension, compounding Pam's horror. Hooper cuts to the rear of Leatherface as he lifts Pam with ease and literally drops her onto the hook.[8] Yet nothing is seen. Hooper chooses not to show the hook entering her back nor the hook violently piercing her chest as it bursts through from the impact. There even isn't a shot of the embedded hook. Instead there is just a shot of Pam, hanging, screaming, trying to free herself.

While Pam flails upon the hook, Hooper explores the details of this kitchen. Blood runs down the walls, collecting in acrid pools; pots and pans remain unwashed, caked in burnt food and more blood. Cutlery and utensils rust and are mixed in with construction tools – different types of hammers, nails, saws. Flies buzz around it all, yet beneath all the splatters of blood and thick grime is a recognisably 'normal' kitchen – a sink, a table, a freezer, cupboards and drawers. Cutlery and cooking implements sit on the draining board, the sink is filled with dirty plates. This underlying mise-en-scène evokes Punter and Byron's observations that the haunted castle is a paradox of domesticity in which 'ordinary life carries on'. For Leatherface, the kitchen is indeed 'normal', a space in which his 'normal' life continues to carry on – he has caught his meal and now, in the kitchen, he is going to prepare it. With such a psychology at work, the kitchen becomes a site in which a union of the 'normal' domestic and the slaughterhouse is taking place for the tools of both spaces merge, as do the key acts of such places – the killing of the cattle, the preparing of a meal. The meat of the cattle – Kirk and Pam – will be butchered in this room. Some will be cooked and later served to the rest of the family. Some will be wrapped and put in the freezer. Domestic life, for Leatherface at least, carries on as normal.

Ignoring Pam's screams, Leatherface carries on with his domestic chores, searching through the various bits of rusting cutlery and implements, throwing them aside or into the filthy sink. He eventually finds what he is looking for, the titular chainsaw. He pulls the ignition cord and lifts it as he revs the engine, the whirring drowning out Pam's screaming. He appears to approach Pam, suggesting that she is to be dismembered but, conspicuously, Kirk's body lies on the kitchen table, his head hanging over the side. Instead of attacking Pam, Leatherface brings the saw down on Kirk and appears to be cutting off his head.

In terms of style and graphic representation, this beheading is as discreet as Pam's impalement. Nothing is seen. There is no blood, no spurting arteries, no severed head dropping to the floor. Just Leatherface lifting his saw and moving it back and forth. The horror, then, comes not from what is actually seen but in what is implied, the rapid accumulation of these assaults, from which the audience is now reeling. It is the act of beheading with a chainsaw that is sickening, a quality compounded by the beheader wearing a mask of human skin and that Pam, still alive and thrashing upon the meat hook, is not only hung before her dead boyfriend but is witness to his dismemberment. The scene functions then as a torture for Pam, indicating that should she not escape then this fate awaits her too. For the audience, all of those bad omens, solar alignments and implications of cannibalism reach their dreadful climax in this scene. Torture, murder, dismemberment, and consumption all collide in this room with the rotten mise-en-scène.

PANIC

By now it is dusk. After some discussion, Jerry decides to look for Kirk and Pam and, following Franklin's directions for the swimming hole, inevitably ends up at Leatherface's house. Lured inside by a series of strange animal sounds, Jerry enters the kitchen area, where he hears a banging from inside the freezer. He opens it and finds Pam inside, crammed in with cling-film-wrapped cuts of meat.[9] As she springs up, shrieking, Leatherface appears out of the shadows, wielding a sledgehammer. Lifting it above his head, he fells Jerry with one blow, just as Franklin described only hours ago in the camper van. It is worth noting that Punter and Byron suggest that with its 'tomb-like claustrophobia' the haunted castle 'enacts the hovering possibility of premature burial' (2004: 262). Pam's incarceration in the freezer carries multiple meanings: it clearly identifies her as meat to be consumed at a later date while the freezer acts as the tomb to her premature burial. (Recalling Punter and Byron's observation that the haunted castle has a propensity for enclosure, within Leatherface's home, Pam is indeed locked away from that fickle memory of 'ordinary life'.)

Having felled Jerry, Leatherface panics. This is odd as, up until now, this hulking figure has demonstrated supreme power and deft control. But with Jerry now convulsing on the floor, Leatherface quickly becomes agitated and searches the kitchen/slaughter room. He runs out and into the feather and bone room, pulling aside the curtains, shrieking incomprehensible words as he goes. He paces up and down as he looks out the window, drops the sledgehammer and throws himself down into one of the chairs, his head in his hands. Hooper cuts to a close-up and the mask is seen in detail (the fragility of the tanned skin, the stitches pulled tight), tongue flicking over his lips and running over his buckled teeth, over and over.

In sharp contrast to the powerful violence that Leatherface has so far exerted, this weirdly comic scene is perhaps the most pivotal in understanding *who* Leatherface actually is. Far from being an impassive, imposing brute force, according to Hooper, Leatherface is actually just 'a big baby' and at this point in the film 'he freaks out because he doesn't know where all the people are coming from' (in *The Shocking Truth*, 2000). Hansen adds that although 'he is the most violent of the characters in the film he's also the most frightened character in the film' (ibid.). This scene then can be read in different ways: it primarily functions as a moment of panic, a culmination of a series of events in which Leatherface's house is not only trespassed upon but seemingly invaded by that most frightening of elements, the outside world. Their entry into his world is, from his perspective, a violation, destroying the illusion of safety his lovingly decorated house represents. The young trespassers shift from invaders to witnesses. In his panic at their appearance, Leatherface instinctively kills them and, by doing so, shifts their status once more to that of cattle for the slaughter. An alternate way of reading the scene would be that Leatherface is, as if in a tar-black sitcom, experiencing a severe domestic crisis. Not only is his house being invaded but, as Hansen has commented, 'dinner won't stay dead' (Jaworzyn, 2003: 41).

LEATHERFACE, THE GREATER MALEFIC

In the semi-darkness of their grandparents' ruin, Sally and her brother argue. Sally wants to look for Jerry while Franklin, still fearing Hitchhiker might return to kill him, refuses to go. Their argument continues until Franklin gives in to Sally (but only because Jerry has the keys to the van) and both go in search of their missing friends. As they approach Leatherface's house, Sally sees a light but Franklin sees movement in the surrounding darkness. Casting the beam of his flashlight into the surroundings, the whirr of the chainsaw is heard and Leatherface lurches out from the darkness and disembowels Franklin.

Given the sum total so far of Leatherface's murderous actions, it is possible to align him with Pam's astrological readings: she states early on in the film that within the timeframe of the narrative Saturn is in retrograde and therefore exerting dangerous and evil influence upon those whose star sign falls within its orbit. In terms of myth, Saturn is the Roman god of agriculture and harvest. Often depicted with a sickle in his left hand and a bundle of wheat in his right, this god, during their positive phase, reigned over a golden age of abundance and peace. When in retrograde that reign is naturally reversed, resulting in a poor harvest and conflict. Given this, we can suggest that Leatherface is a contemporary representation of this myth: living in rural Texas, his employment, prior to mechanisation, was within the industry of agriculture, and he wields not a scythe but a lump hammer, sledge hammer and chain saw. Because the events of the film take place when Saturn is in retrograde it is unsurprising that this representation of a mythical god is going to engage in conflict. He is further associated and connected to the symbolic properties of Saturn in that the planet is constantly associated with death, an obvious correlative in that Leatherface is actually the only character in the film who kills (despite his brothers' cannibalistic tastes and his grandfather's attempt to assault Sally, none of them actual kill any of the teenagers). He is, in effect, the physical embodiment of Death in this narrative.

ENDNOTES

1. The other parameters defined by Punter and Byron are the Vampire, Female Gothic, the Uncanny, the History of Abuse, Hallucination and the Narcotic.

2. The Gothic nature of *The Texas Chain Saw Massacre* is pre-empted early on in the film when the group decide to pick up Hitchhiker: once he is inside the van, Franklin looks at him and comments to his sister and friends, 'I think we just picked up Dracula'. Upon hearing Hitchhiker's stories about his family he adds to this comment, '[They're] a whole family of Draculas'. As humorous as Franklin's comments may be, his description of Hitchhiker and his family clearly equates one of Gothic's most notable creations with their acts of slaughter – both Dracula and the *Chain Saw* clan live by literally feeding off the innocent.

3. In terms of style, obscurity is a further visual trait within the film. This manifests itself in a number of different ways, from the long-shot in the graveyard as Sally walks to her grandfather's grave (her progress concealed behind the many tombstones), to shots that look through semi-transparent surfaces, such as the wet windscreen of the camper van when the frail petrol station attendant washes it, obscuring his facial features to the extent that they look deformed (suggesting that given his manager is Cook, this person is a hunched surrogate for the much stronger but equally disfigured Leatherface), or the mesh screen through which Pam and Jerry look through into Leatherface's house. In more blatant terms, obscurity is one of the functions of Leatherface's mask – to conceal his (presumed) deformity and so give him a 'new' and 'perfectly formed' face.

4. It should be noted that Franklin isn't the only one to find further portents of doom: Kirk wanders through the Hardesty house alone and, upon entering one of the upstairs rooms, finds a corner dominated by a nest of swarming spiders, their presence seemingly 'devouring' the room through their numbers.

5. (Rick Worland comments that the construction of scenes leading to Kirk and Pam's murder implies nudity and a sex scene but this never happens. Instead, both are brutally murdered without any nudity occurring at all. This absence of both nudity and sex scene is later underscored by Sally's ordeal at the dining table: 'Sally hysterically offers to submit to any perverse sex acts they desire in exchange for her life, she is met with virtual incomprehension, so fully committed is the family to pointless terrorising and ultimately, cannibalism' (2007: 217–218).

6. Pam's kicking of the bucket is a joke, as she is about to die, to figuratively 'kick the bucket'.

7. The reason why Gunnar Hansen was chosen by Hooper to play the part of Leatherface was because of his sheer bulk: 'Tobe told me that as soon as I arrived for the [audition] he decided to give me the part, because I filled the door!' (Gunnar Hansen in Bradley, 2004: 163).

8. It could be argued that this penetration connects with the skull and cattle horn totem: in both, a human is violently pierced with a sharp, curved object, both suspended from the

ceiling. In this respect Pam, in her torture, becomes a living totem, her agonised thrashing causing her body to slowly rotate.

9. Mark Bould equates Pam's entrapment with the chicken she saw in the room of feather and bone, stating 'the strange image of the fatted chicken, stuffed into a cage like a ship in a bottle; appropriately, Pam, who finds it, is crammed – still alive – into a freezer' (2003: 108).

REFERENCES

Bould, M., 2003. Apocalypse Here and Now: Making Sense of The Texas Chain Saw Massacre. In: G. D. Rhodes, ed. 2003. Horror at the Drive-in: Essays in Popular Americana. Jefferson, N.C.: McFarland & Co. pp. 97–112.

Bradley, D., 2004. Behind the Mask of the Horror Actor. London: Titan Books.

Jaworzyn, S., 2003. The Texas Chain Saw Massacre Companion. London: Titan Books.

Punter, D. & Byron, G., 2004. The Gothic. Oxford: Blackwell Publishing.

Sawyers Chainsaw Page, n.d. Quotes from Tobe Hooper [Online]
http://www.angelfire.com/in/sawyerschainsawpage/index7.html [Accessed 23 March 2012].

The Shocking Truth, 2000. [Film] Directed by David Gregory. USA: Exploited Film.

Worland, R., 2007. The Horror Film: An Introduction. Oxford: Blackwell Publishing.

THE FAMILY

While the motifs of the haunted castle and the monster dominate *The Texas Chain Saw Massacre*, its Gothic potential is compounded by the film's final third, in which the entire narrative is given over to the persecution of Sally. This concept has only presented itself briefly in the first half of the film, manifested most clearly in the assault upon Pam. Punter and Byron suggest that the key elements of this trope are:

> … the uncertainties of character positioning and instabilities of knowledge. Far from knowing everything, [protagonistic characters] frequently know little or nothing about the world through which they move or about the structures of power which envelop them… [These people are] persecuted victims, subject to violence and pursuit for incomprehensible reasons. (2004: 273)

Pam's entry into Leatherface's house and into the room of feather and bone is, for her, quite literally stumbling into a different world, one that is, as has been discussed, a fabrication of an insane mindset. Here, in this world, the power structures that govern the 'normal' world of Law and Order have descended into a chaos of torture, mutilation and murder. In this insanity, Pam is enveloped by the powerful Leatherface and dragged screaming into his world, while Kirk is almost instantly killed by that same powerful force. Both Pam and Kirk 'know little' about this man and why he is ultimately doing what he does. His chainsawing of Kirk and his impalement of Pam are incompressible to them – they have done nothing wrong, only entered into his property looking for petrol. It would seem, to them at least, that they are being violently persecuted simply for *being*. This descent into an insane power structure and subjection to the incomprehensible (or, as the opening narration describes it, 'the mad and the macabre') has only really just begun by this point in the film; its full manifestation will come later when Sally sits at the dining table with Leatherface and his family.

Having watched her brother be disembowelled, Sally runs. Leatherface chases her through the dark, the whine of his chain saw merging with Sally's incessant screams. Through the trees she sees a house and, still screaming, runs to its back door. Unable to get anyone's attention – and with Leatherface now close behind – she runs around to the front of the house, opens the door and goes inside. As she slams the front door, the interior of the hallway is revealed to the audience – the wallpaper peels from the walls, its edge curling around the many animal skins that adorn the stairwell. Sally has mistakenly entered Leatherface's home. Hearing the chain saw approaching, Sally runs up the stairs and enters a chamber of horror.

As has been indicated in the previous chapter, the haunted castle of Gothic narratives is a space in which time and history has collapsed, a location in which the present rests uneasily alongside elements of the past. Entering into one of the upstairs rooms, Sally sees a seated couple. In her fear, she fails to notice the lampshade, the only light source in the room, is made of stacked human vertebrae. She stumbles forward, falling at the knees of an old man. Grabbing his hands she asks for help but soon realises that she is holding onto what appears to be a corpse. She turns, her feet knocking over the skeleton of dog, its skin draped over the bones. In the other chair, wearing an ill-fitting wig and dust-grey dress, is the desiccated corpse of a woman. It is a disturbing arrangement, one in which the wholesome domestic image of grandfather and grandmother sitting before the open fire, their pet curled up at their feet, is grotesquely re-enacted. It would seem, from this room alone, that the upper levels of this slaughterhouse are still moments in time, frozen snapshots from the past populated by the corpses of family members. Heritage lingers while memory remains intact in this sickening tableaux. In Leatherface's haunted castle, then, the dead are not buried but *preserved*, their remains left to slowly dry out in the intense Texas heat. These corpses become both totems and relics, fragments of Leatherface's lineage, his assumed ancestry that he cannot let go of. These corpses and his masks of human skin all indicate a preoccupation that is not overtly with cannibalism but with preservation, a desire to suspend time, if not stop it. Perhaps it was Leatherface himself who drove the nail through the pocket watch and hung it outside his house – here, the desire is not ultimately for the flesh but to stop time, dead.

Downstairs, Leatherface is attempting to cut through the front door with the chain saw. Screaming, Sally runs down the stairs as he manages to break through. In an almost comedic moment, Sally double takes, screams some more, turns and runs back up the stairs. Leatherface gives chase but Sally runs the length of the landing and leaps out of the end window. She looks up and Leatherface is grinding his saw against the broken frame, seemingly trapped. She slowly gets up and begins to limp away but the saw is heard again and Leatherface appears out the darkness and gives chase once more.

The only woman seen in Leatherface's family - the desiccated remains of Grandma.

The pursuit concludes when Sally sees another light, this time the petrol station she and her friends stopped at earlier that day. Falling (once again) into the space, Sally is picked up by the petrol station owner who warned Kirk and Jerry some hours ago. Managing to calm her down, he establishes what has happened and reassures her there is no one outside. Sally asks him to phone the police but he says there isn't a phone and so they must drive to the nearest town. Reassuring her once more, he leaves to get his truck. While he is gone, Sally stares at portions of meat which cook on a grill in the corner of the office: Hooper intercuts a slow zoom into Sally face, from medium close-up to close-up, with an identical zoom into the meat. The cross-cutting is clear in its intentions – that the meat is human flesh and that Sally, should she not escape from the petrol station owner, will soon be butchered herself and served up from that grill. Compounding this is the soundtrack. As each zoom gets closer to the subject, the diegetic sound increases, the sound of the meat sizzling on the grill mingling with the news announcement playing the background. The broadcast, perhaps unsurprisingly given the intercutting, is about the grave robberies that took place the night before. The report places emphasis on the acts of dismemberment that have taken place, the detailed removing of limbs and extremities visually echoed in the shapes of the cooking meat.

The petrol station owner pulls his pick-up truck next to the entrance and gets out, a sack and a length of rope in his hands. Sally asks him what he is doing as he approaches her. As he tries to calm her, Sally grabs a knife from by the cooking meat and attempts to defend herself but is disarmed when the station owner knocks it from her hand with a broom handle. He beats Sally some more, the force of the blows breaking the broom in two, until she is unconscious. He then ties her arms behind her back, gags her with a filthy rag and puts the sack over her head and torso. Taking her to the truck, he puts her in the front passenger seat and goes to drive away but stops. He gets out and returns to the station to switch off the lights and lock the entrance door. Getting back into the truck he comments to Sally that he 'had to lock up and get the lights. The cost of electricity is enough to drive a man out of business'.

While this line of dialogue offers an amusing, if not sharp, contrast to the violent events Sally is experiencing, it also directs attention to another of the film's subtextual elements: as noted by Naomi Merritt, a number of scholarly texts concerning *The Texas Chain Saw Massacre* have noted that 'the excesses of capitalism [is] a source of [the film's] horror' (2010: 204), with Merritt citing Robin Wood, Tony Williams and Kendall R. Phillips as prime exponents of this reading. Wood, for example, states that 'cannibalism represents… the logical end of human relations under capitalism' (1979: 189) for the consumer has turned upon consumer and, quite literally, *consumed* them. Cannibalism has become not just a breaking of a taboo but simply the basest and most extreme form of consumerism. For Merritt, the film presents:

> [a] horrific parody of American values, [where] the film's theme of 'cannibalistic capitalism' plays out the tensions borne of the historical and political circumstances of the period of the film's production. The far-from triumphant end of the Vietnam War, the loss of confidence in political authority and integrity following the Watergate scandal, the oil crisis (which disrupted the lives of ordinary car-driving Americans) leading into a major stock market crash and recession, were among a number of challenges to the American 'way of life' in the early to mid 1970s. (2010: 202–203)

From this perspective the film's underlying rationale for the murders and subsequent cannibalism are reinstated – without employment, Leatherface and his family simply 'direct their idle skills towards the butchery of humans' (ibid: 203).

Such a political reading of the film polarises the petrol station owner's comment: flesh has simply become a freely available commodity to Leatherface and his family in such straightened times. By murdering they have debased themselves to committing the ultimate taboo without any guilt or remorse, yet given their poverty, their concerns lie not with discovery, capture and imprisonment but their next utilities payment.

TORMENT AND PERSECUTION

For Sally the seemingly trustworthy adult figure of the petrol station owner proves to be unreliable, a source not of help but further victimisation. The station owner fluctuates from being a caring and supportive figure to a malicious and violent figure, simultaneously offering to help only to immediately inflict punishment. There is a strong element of sadism to his punishments – his initial beating of Sally is punctuated by sniggers and laughter and a manic grin. His dances around Sally as if he were a child, gleefully hitting her as if it were some sort of vindictive game. The beatings become increasingly violent, slipping from child-like torment to aggressive adult violence as he towers over her, hitting her, his face taut with anger. The sadistic beatings continue in the car with the station owner once again both calming Sally with soothing words of comfort only to then poke and hit her with the broken remains of the broom handle. While it is clear that this man does not want to kill Sally just yet, it is also evident that this intention will be a long time coming. It would seem that there is much pleasure to be gained from the capture and torment of cattle, that fun can be had with those who do not understand what is going to happen to them.

The truck turns down a driveway and, in the poor illumination of the headlights, a figure is seen dancing along the path, its arms flying in cartwheels around its head and body. The station owner mutters 'half wit' partly to himself and perhaps in part to Sally. The headlights fall fully upon the figure and we have returned to the scenario that opened the film, a truck pulling over to pick up Hitchhiker. This time, however, the station owner gets out and almost immediately begins beating Hitchhiker with the broken broom handle, cursing him and shouting 'I told you to stay away from that graveyard'. The ambiguities and suggestions from earlier are now beginning to make sense – Hitchhiker is indeed the anonymous figure who was committing the exhumations and creating those 'grisly works of art'. And it would seem that both Hitchhiker and petrol station owner know each other, as, while administering the beating, the station owner says, 'I told you to never leave your brother alone'. Given the behaviour that these men have so far exhibited, we now realise it is likely that the 'brother' will be Leatherface and that the station owner is either their hard- working, bread-winning father or elder brother who has assumed patriarchal status. Hitchhiker gets into the back of the pick-up as it drives onward towards a familiar house, the front door ajar and severely damaged.

ATTEMPTING CONTAINMENT, ATTEMPTING SPEECH

The station owner and Hitchhiker get Sally out of the truck and drag her to the porch. Upon seeing the damage caused to the front door, the station owner almost hysterically screams 'look what your brother did to the door!'. His berating continues and culminates in 'He has no pride in his home!'. While these lines of dialogue are delivered in a comedic manner, they also point towards a subtle recurrent element within the film – containment: in her text *Access and Excess in The Texas Chain Saw Massacre* (2010), Lucy Fife Donaldson suggests that virtually all the characters within the film are subject to broaching an imposed sense of containment: the teenagers drive off the highway and down deserted tracks (despite being told not to) and then later split up when they should stay together, the station owner's attempts to control Hitchhiker fail who, in turn, refuses to stay at home and look after Leatherface, instead leaving him alone so that he can indulge in grave robbery. These failed attempts at control extend into the spaces of containment as Leatherface leaves the house (when he shouldn't) to pursue Sally: Sally escapes from his house by leaping out of a window; Sally is bound and gagged and thrown into a truck and then later tied to a chair; the sacrosanct space of the containing grave is broached by Hitchhiker. The control of containment then is almost virtually lost as each instance fails and chaos is set free.

In contrast to his own broaching of containment, Leatherface enforces a sense of crude containment in his response to the trespass of the teenagers: he successfully traps Pam inside the freezer, despite Jerry's attempts to free her, while his murder of Kirk, Pam, Jerry and Franklin are his way of trying to ensure containment. By killing all four teenagers he is able to control events and ensure that they are never able to speak of what the intruders have witnessed and experienced.

As Hitchhiker and the station owner struggle to get Sally into the house, Leatherface appears in the hallway. Wearing his Old Lady mask, he walks out to greet them but is quickly chased back into the kitchen by the station owner. Brandishing the broken broom handle, he shouts out 'You damn fool! You ruined the door!' Leatherface cowers in the corner as the station owner stands before him, the broom handle held high. He asks if he caught the other teenagers, to which Leatherface responds with a series of squeals and grunts. The man seems to understand these sounds and lowers the broom handle.

It is worth noting that an ability to speak is identified by Punter and Byron as a significant area for understanding the Gothic monster. They state that a range of Gothic texts preoccupied with the monster demonstrate sympathy for this character by allowing them 'to speak and explain the origins of [their] monstrous behaviour' (2004: 265). While the feeling of sympathy for Leatherface is perhaps virtually void (despite the beratings and beatings he receives), he does have, in some sense, the capacity to express himself verbally: in the original drafts of the script, Leatherface had dialogue:

> The lines in the script had meaning. I wrote down what those lines were supposed to mean. And we sat down and ran those lines, we shot the scene and Tobe said, 'It doesn't work, there's too much intelligence in the character.' So we redid it. Leatherface knows what he wants to say but he can't get his mouth to say the right sounds. He has the idea of speech, but he can't express it – he just makes sounds randomly thinking that it means something. (Gunnar Hansen in Jaworzyn, 2003: 43)

To all intents and purpose then, Leatherface can *speak* and express himself yet he does not explain why he is murdering these people. Instead, his squeals and grunts translate, according to Hansen, as attempts to either gain approval or integrate verbally with the events that surround him:

Iba goba igee em a.	I've been a good boy and I got 'em all.
Li o ba fu gapa gil.	You can do it Grandpa, kill her.
Aba do hil li ito giba giba.	That'll do it, let her have it, get her.

The above are Hansen translations (ibid.) of the dialogue Hoper and Henkel scripted for Leatherface. While they do not provide any form of rationale or commentary into why he is killing the teenagers, they do provide a personal idioglassia: defined as a private language which is often constructed by children, Hansen's translations support Hooper's assertion that Leatherface is nothing more than 'a big baby', who desires to be a 'normal' part of the group that he lives with. His voice then acts like the masks of flayed skin – they are both approximates, attempts that simultaneously function as an act of becoming 'normal' through mimicry – the mimicry of a 'normal' face, the mimicry of a 'normal' voice.

By now Sally has been dragged into the dining room and tied to a chair by Hitchhiker. They take off the sack and take out the gag. The petrol station owner, who has now been identified as Cook, sends Hitchhiker upstairs to 'get your Grandpa'. He then stands over Sally and, once again, tries to calm her but Leatherface appears, curiously looking over Cook's shoulder at her. Cook turns upon him and, threatening him the with broom handle, orders him back into the kitchen. Hitchhiker returns with Grandpa, who is, predictably, the assumed corpse Sally encountered when she first ran into the house. Sitting opposite her, it becomes apparent that the old man is alive. Leatherface cuts open Sally's finger and forces it into Grandpa's mouth. As he feverishly sucks upon her finger, Sally passes out. When she comes round, Sally is at the head of the dining table, the four men eating their evening meal. Realising she is awake, they begin a long night of torture, teasing and abusing Sally until they decide that she should be killed, the honour of which goes to Grandpa. Forcing her head over a metal bucket, Leatherface gives Grandpa a lump hammer. In an excruciating scene that is both tense and comic, the old man repeatedly drops the hammer until he final manages one, glancing blow. Frustrated, Hitchhiker takes up the hammer but in the ensuing argument over who will kill her, Sally manages to escape. Running down the room she once more jumps out of a window and to her assumed freedom.

THE FAMILY

It is clear from the way in which the three men speak to each other that they are, in one way or another, a family. From the point at which Cook first sees Hitchhiker in the headlights, a family structure is implied and, to a certain extent, played out during the climatic scenes of Sally's torture: Cook has taken on the role of the father who goes out to work to earn money for his family, Hitchhiker is the wayward teenager who refuses to do as he is told, while Leatherface is the mother who is stuck in the kitchen and subject to some domestic abuse from her 'husband' Cook. Such a dynamic suggests a patriarchal power structure within this family, a quality compounded by Cook's judicious delivery of punishment with the broken broom handle, hitting, as he does, both Hitchhiker and Leatherface for their various misdemeanours. While this power structure is evident during Cook's arrival at the family home, it slowly starts to shift when the family begins their torture of Sally. For the most part, Cook seems simultaneously to be horrified by the acts being committed at the same time as appearing to enjoy them, with his dialogue expressing this schizophrenic reaction: 'You're beyond help, lady' is contrasted with 'No need to torture the poor girl' and 'I just can't take no pleasure in killing'. As the psychological torture inflicted upon Sally increases, Cook moves away from the table, reluctant to get involved or even witness the acts Hitchhiker and Leatherface inflict upon her. Yet, when Grandpa is given the lump hammer, he quickly rejoins the group, verbalising to Sally a further contradictory statement in that 'Grandpa was the best killer there ever was. Why it took no more than one lick they say. He did six in five minutes once… Grandpa's the best, it won't hurt a bit'. Here Cook completely reneges his position of Father to the Grandfather, allowing the older generation the glory of the kill and, through his dialogue, not only celebrates his grandfather's skill but perversely reassures Sally that her tortures will soon be over, as will her life, with one quick blow.

Given the presence of the four men, an obvious observation regarding this family is the absence of any female family members. The only possible female relative who is seen, the corpse that Sally finds seated opposite Grandpa, is dead. With her antiquated clothes and jewellery and her placement opposite Grandpa it could be assumed that this is indeed Grandma; but strangely, mother and father are inexplicably absent from this family of cannibals. The reason for this absence remains ambiguous in the film – they are never mentioned in the characters' dialogue nor are they ever seen, either physically or through framed imagery upon the decaying walls of the family home. Instead they are simply absent. Perhaps the audience is to assume that their mother and father are dead, possibly murdered and eaten by their children but such an assumption does contrast with the brothers' strong sense of family unity, so such a possibility is perhaps unlikely.

Without a mother in the household, Leatherface has taken this role upon himself for he is the one who wears the masks of women's skin, the one who wears the apron, the one who works in the kitchen to prepare the family meals. As Gunnar Hansen has stated:

> in effect Leatherface is saying 'Well, we need a woman around the house now' because he's obviously taken on the role of the housekeeper. He's been in the kitchen making dinner so he's taking on the mother role'. (Jaworzyn, 2003: 41)

With Leatherface as Mother, the earlier scenes involving Leatherface are polarised by this gender role: the masks do not operate to conceal or induce fear but *provide* an identity and so work to feminise this huge, muscular man. This contrast between feminine face and masculine bulk reoccurs in both Leatherface's apron and chain saw – in his first appearance the apron is a blood-splattered part of his slaughterhouse uniform but by the narrative's end it is a feminine item of clothing, a 'dress' to wear while cooking in the kitchen while his chain saw (that most powerful, masculine and phallic of power tools) is reduced to the status of another kitchen implement, found as it is among the knives, forks, spoons and whisks within the kitchen. Consequently, Leatherface is emasculated, which, consequently serves to confuse his identity further. Instead of been fixed as simply the narrative's monster, his masks, clothes, actions and status within the aberrant family unit creates a confusion of possible identities that ultimately remains unresolved: he is, at any given time: a savage protector of the family property, a frightened child who speaks his own fabricated language, a skilled butcher, a housekeeper, a cook, and a mother.

The only living woman within the household is Sally. By being placed at the head of the dining table, Mark Bould suggests that 'the slaughterhouse family wish to incorporate [her] both literally, by ingestion, and metaphorically, by offering her the seat at the table belonging to the missing wife-mother' (2003: 100). This reading adds a further perversity to the dining sequence, for if Sally is indeed positioned (albeit temporarily) as Mother, she becomes the *ultimate* provider of nourishment for the family – instead of preparing and cooking food, she *is* the food: when her finger is cut open and bleed, it becomes a perverse breast, a nipple upon which Grandpa literally (and disturbingly) suckles while upon her death, her flesh will be butchered, cooked and ingested by the family of men.

In both situations, Sally is rendered as Mother through her body but not by her sexuality. At no point in the dining sequence is her sexuality a concern of the men. Such is the extent of this is that when Sally pleads to them by saying 'Please, I'll do anything you want' the men look at her in a confused disgust. She has clearly misunderstood the desires of these men. Such is their perversity or descent into primitivism, that sex and sexuality have lost their function and meaning, resulting in sexuality being perverted, as Robin Wood suggests, 'into sadism, violence and cannibalism'. Wood continues by acknowledging that 'it is striking that there is no suggestion anywhere that Sally is the object of an overtly sexual threat: she is to be tortured, killed, dismembered, eaten, but not raped' (1979: 189).

In his book *Hearths of Darkness: The Family in the American Horror Film*, Tony Williams[1] has identified, that:

> … during the 1970s an unusual event affected Hollywood's representation of the American family. Generally revered as a positive icon of 'normal' human society, the institution underwent severe assault. (1996: 13)

Williams indicates that the antagonist of these assaults was neither external nor a contemporary manifestation of the monsters from the classic era of American horror cinema but from a threat that 'came from within' (1996: 13). Williams cites *Night of the Living Dead* (1968), *Rosemary's Baby* (1968), *The Exorcist* (1973), *Its Alive* (1973), and *The Omen* (1976) as prime examples, before stating that:

> In *The Last House on the Left* (1972), *The Texas Chain Saw Massacre* (1974) and *The Hills Have Eyes* (1977), typical American families encounter their monstrous counterparts, undergo (or perpetuate) brutal violence, and eventually survive with the full knowledge of their kinship to their monstrous counterparts (ibid.).

Williams' observation of the mirrored family[2] is first intimated at the start of the film when a shared sense of ancestry is verbalised by Franklin: 'Hey, that's where Grandpa used to sell his cattle'. His observation seems a little redundant so early on in the film, but upon the revelation of Grandpa – 'the best killer there was' – a generational connection is made between the two families in that both Sally's grandfather and Leatherface's Grandpa were connected to the same location, the slaughterhouse. It is interesting to note that it is Franklin who makes this observation, for throughout the film he is the one who recalls and verbalises the past and makes the connections between the past and the present. Under this context, his verbal interaction with Hitchhiker takes on a different perspective in that Franklin seems to recognise in Hitchhiker a sense of his own family heritage, that through questioning Hitchhiker and through looking at his Polaroid photographs he can gain an insight into his own family's past.

The connection between the two soon extends into Williams' reading, in that Hitchhiker and Franklin are the mirror of each other: both talk in an animated fashion about the slaughter of cattle, with Franklin asking with child-like glee about which is the most effective means of slaughter and enquiring into how the carcasses were butchered. In this enthusiastic dialogue, Franklin and Hitchhiker are presented as equals and paralleled as the camera cuts back and forth between the two in which is essentially the same head-and-shoulders shot. While this visually connects them as equals, the drawing of blood unifies them symbolically: borrowing Franklin's penknife, Hitchhiker cuts open his own palm and returns the knife. Upon the ritual burning of Franklin's photograph, he draws his own cut-throat razor and slices open Franklin's forearm. Although the wounds are not pressed together, the act of cutting becomes a symbolic union between them: Hitchhiker is bled by Franklin's knife and vice versa. This sense of symmetry is reflected in that both have a fresh injury to their arm and both are disabled in some way – Franklin is confined to his wheelchair while Hitchhiker is 'disfigured' by the deep red birth mark that runs the length of his face. Later, when Franklin and Kirk are left alone in the van, Franklin asks Kirk if he could cut himself like Hitchhiker did and then in a further unifying act, mimics the cutting open of his own palm.

Williams extends his reading by suggesting that, in contrast to his strong connection with Hitchhiker, Franklin can also be aligned with Leatherface, in that 'Sally has to look after him as Hitchhiker has to care for Leatherface. Both siblings resent this family duty' (1996: 189–190). He later comments that both are 'obese, unwholesome, dependent children within their families' (1996: 192). In this reflection, Sally becomes Hitchhiker, solely through a seemingly parentally enforced sibling care, an act which prevents both from doing what they want to: Hitchhiker is made housebound by his responsibilities to his brother while Sally, guiltily, takes Franklin along with her and her friends for the day trip. Either way, the brother becomes a burden of responsibility and a barrier to enjoyment (as perverse as that may be for Hitchhiker). In this respect, the earlier idea of containment is in some way transformed into impediment as both Sally and Hitchhiker are restrained by their respective brothers, each needing a different type of care and attention.

EATING DINNER

Coming around, Sally finds herself at the dining table. It is decorated with human skulls, animals shells and assorted bones. Flies buzz lazily in the air and Leatherface, now dressed in a suit and tie and wearing the Pretty Woman mask, stares intently at her. She screams and, in seemingly joyous union, the three brothers join in with howls and whoops and screams of their own. So begins Sally's long night of torture and persecution: having begun with the lies and beatings from Cook, she is tied to a chair whose arm rests are, literally, severed arms; a cut-throat razor is held to her throat, she is repeatedly mocked by Hitchhiker; and her face stroked by Leatherface as he admires her skin. Given the earlier suggestions that both families are made up of children, the persecution Sally endures takes on a childish quality, reworking Sally's torture into the psychological abuse of a childish game in which the ugly boys torment the pretty young girl while Leatherface's protracted pursuit of her becomes a perversely simple game of chase. At its most intense, this childish behaviour is intensely expressed when Sally screams in sheer despair when her attempts to reason with the men are mocked, and Hitchhiker, leaning close to her, sticks out his bottom lip in a sad mimicry before sarcastically shouting 'Boo hoo hoo'. Here the children bully and tease, mock and torment.

Her entire experience with the family of men is a condensation of Punter and Byron's descriptor of Gothic persecution because, like Kirk, Pam and Jerry before her, she has no understanding of what is happening to her, or why. Her ordeal becomes simply a series of physical and psychological tortures for no apparent reason, a quality emphasised by the men's rejection of her offer to sexually satisfy each of them. For them, this is about fun before murder, a grotesquely amusing opportunity to play with their food before they eat it. Sally is rendered powerless in the face of this abuse: she is unable to free the ties that bind her to the dining chair, nor is she able to barter for her freedom with sexual favours. Instead, she is enveloped by the insane power of the family, subject to their abuse and torments to the extent that she herself descends into an insane state. Retreating in this manner, Sally's Gothic persecution is complete: her rational self dissolves, surrendering both body and mind to the incompressible forces that surround her.

Her torture reaches its crescendo when it is decided that Grandpa should be the one to kill her. As already noted, Cook both frightens her and comforts her when he tells of his Grandpa's legendary ability to kill cattle with a single 'lick' of the hammer. Untied and with her head forced over a metal bucket, Leatherface puts the lump hammer into Grandpa's pale, wrinkled hand, but each time he drops it. The dull *clunk* of metal against metal is a further grotesque amusement as much as it is a visualisation of the fate that awaits Sally. The attempts to hit her continue, with each blow either missing completely or the hammer falling into the bucket. The protraction is painful: Sally screams and attempts to escape, Grandpa tries to hold the hammer, all the while Leatherface and Hitchhiker getting increasingly frustrated. Grandpa manages one hit, the hammer breaking the surface of the skin and causing it to bleed a little – but for all of Cook's expounding of his grandfather's craft, this is hardly a death blow. In this moment, the past and the present violently collide: by allowing Grandpa the opportunity to deliver the killer blow, Leatherface and his brothers engage not only a ritualistic murder but also use the act of killing as a further celebration of their ancestry. Grandpa, the legendary killer, is given the opportunity to demonstrate his skill and prove to this innocent victim of the present that the Old Ways still live on and that they are still effective. Yet Grandpa fails, repeatedly, to kill her. It becomes a joke not on Sally but upon Leatherface and his family; the Old Ways are failing. As Christopher Sharrett states:

> Grandpa is remembered as the best killer in the slaughterhouse; there is no irony that Grandpa, the wizened ruler of the wasteland, is given the job of killing Sally and drops the hammer. (1983: 271)

The sustained persecution of Sally raises a further reference to the Gothic: her narrative trajectory and the horror she experiences within it are all indicative of the female Gothic. Punter and Byron briefly describe a possible definition of this sub-genre as one which 'typically represents a female protagonist's attempts to escape from a confining interior' (2004: 278) before providing a more complex elaboration:

> In the female Gothic plot, the transgressive male becomes the primary threat to the
> female protagonist. Initially, she is usually depicted enjoying an idyllic and secluded life;
> this is followed by a period of imprisonment when she is confined to a great house
> or castle under the authority of a powerful male figure or his female surrogate. Within
> this labyrinthine space she is trapped and pursued, and the threat may variously be to
> her virtue or to her life. (ibid: 279)

This descriptor clearly articulates Sally's experiences within the film,[3] even to the
correlation of descriptive terms: Sally's narrative begins, as the solemn narrator
describes at the opening of the film, on 'an idyllic summer afternoon'. The descriptor
also places great emphasis upon a dominating male/masculine/patriarchal power. In
Chain Saw this could variously apply to Hitchhiker or Cook, for it is they who capture
her, tie her to a chair and torment her. To suggest they are 'powerful male figure(s)' is,
in part, undermined by their physical appearance for both are slight and thin, tall and
gangly, insane and physically weak yet they *are* powerful figures through the physical
manifestation and/or projection of their aberrant psychologies. Masculine power in *Chain
Saw*, then, if it is considered to be similar to female Gothic narrative tropes, lies not in
physical strength but in insanity. It is a power which is embodied within them, extending
outward to engulf the house and those who enter or are dragged into its orbit. Such a
reading is compounded by Grandpa who, again, is physically weak (he can barely hold
the lump hammer, let alone hit Sally with any effect) but exerts a tremendous influence
as his patriarchal power still holds sway over his grandchildren and which, in turn, is
exerted upon Sally when he attempts to slaughter her. Masculine power becomes
Family Power, an insanity that is passed on from one generation to the next, driving
them inextricably forward into chaos and enabling them to survive and thrive.

While his siblings may be weak, Leatherface is a potent symbol of masculine power, for
he *is* physically strong. While this offers some point of interest, it is of more value to
consider Leatherface as the transgressive male who straddles gender boundaries. As
Punter and Byron state, the threat to the female protagonist is 'a powerful male figure or
his female surrogate' [ibid: 279]. These two types are collapsed into one in Leatherface
through his brute strength, his wearing of masks made from female skin and in his

adopted role as Mother. His appearance, physical strength and allocated role within his family positions him as a dreadful manifestation of the female Gothic threat combined: he is a powerful masculine figure who is at the same time the female surrogate within his masculine family. This quality is compounded by the fact that he appears to desire not only Sally's flesh but also the skin from her face: his caressing of her face while she sits bound to the dining room chair could simply imply an attraction to her but given his predilection for female faces it would indicate a desire to flay and then wear her face. If this is Leatherface's intention then by wearing her face he *will* look like her. This assuming of Sally's identity potentially creates a perverse reversal, for if Leatherface does desire her face then, by wearing it, the powerful, transgressive male transgresses even further by taking upon the appearance of the persecuted victim. This generates two readings: by wearing the face of those his family have tortured and persecuted, Leatherface expresses his own persecution at the hands of his brothers and *becomes*, in appearance, one of their victims himself. In sharp contrast to this, the wearing of the victim's face becomes a trophy of the kill, a worn skin which, although temporarily shifting his gender appearance, functions more as a potent symbol of empowerment which invests him with further strength.

DAWN

Having managed to escape, Sally limps down the driveway, Hitchhiker and Leatherface chasing her. Both brandish weapons – Leatherface holds his revving chain saw above his head, while Hitchhiker lashes out at Sally with his cut-throat razor. Just as Sally reaches the road, Hitchhiker takes hold of her and slashes at her back, intent on once more maiming her so that he may continue his torture. As they struggle, a truck appears and distracts Hitchhiker. Once again Sally escapes and Hitchhiker is crushed by the truck. The driver gets out but is confronted by Leatherface who now, enraged by his brother's death, chases them both. The driver throws a wrench at him, knocking Leatherface over, the chain saw landing on his leg and cutting through to the bone. The driver runs away and Sally flags down a passing pick-up. Bloody and screaming, she crawls into the vehicle. As it drives away her screams become laughter as she watches Leatherface spinning wildly in circles, his chain saw held aloft, against the rising sun.

Given the film's ending it is worth returning to the suggestion that *Chain Saw* shares strong similarities with the narrative trajectories of the female Gothic. While these connections have been discussed earlier, the consequences of Sally's escape from Leatherface and his siblings is in sharp contrast to the relatively fixed conclusion of most female Gothic texts:

> … it is the heroine's experiences which become the focus of attention, and her experiences are represented as a journey leading towards some kind of agency and power in the patriarchal world. (Punter and Byron, 2004: 279)

In genre terms, then, Sally should exit the female Gothic of *Chain Saw* not only alive but also empowered with some sense of dominion over her patriarchal tormentors. But, as it is, Sally exits the narrative as a hysterical, if not insane, individual. Her journey has not led to empowerment or even just a greater understanding of herself but instead has taken her down a singular route into madness and chaos. Her experience within it and her eventually exit from it offers her no agency or power, just a dreadful regression into a hysterical condition. Whereas Punter and Byron allude to the fact that the imprisonments and punishments endured by the protagonist within the female Gothic are the means by which female characters can become empowered emotionally,

Leatherface dances, out of frustration or joy, his chainsaw swinging wildly.

intellectually and physically, Sally's torments show her nothing but the depths of depravity to which individuals can descend. Ultimately, she learns nothing: she is reduced to merely flesh by the antagonists and to a witness by the narrative itself. She is given no agency and no power, managing only to escape because the boys bicker so intensely that they almost forget she is there. In the end Sally has to rely on luck, chance and her own dwindling strength as an individual to propel her out of the nightmare into daylight. And even then, physically and emotionally damaged, she needs to flag down help in the form of masculine symbols – the large, powerful semi-truck and the cowboy driving his pick-up truck.

The film's final image is one of the most powerful in the history of horror cinema. In the maddening spinning, Leatherface is injured but alive. His crazed dance is ambiguous in its purpose, for it is potentially as much a celebration of his freedom as it may be an intense expression of his frustration at Sally's escape. Either way, there is no comfortable resolution: the threat remains at large, a violent serial killer whose transgressions will continue long after the credits have rolled. Unrestrained and unchecked, Leatherface's dance merges him with the sun, absorbing him into its intense orange glow. There, in this consummation, he is finally aligned with the narrative's prime motif of chaos, with the arcane movements of the solar system defining him as an unfathomable and uncontrollable power, one governed by forces beyond the reaches of Law and Order. He is indeed, the grisly work of art, the mad and the macabre, the nightmare and the tragedy.

ENDNOTES

1. Within his discussion on *The Texas Chain Saw Massacre*, Williams suggests that Leatherface's family's penchant for human flesh is a manifestation of the Puritan fear of the Native American Indian and so indicates a genre reading of *Chain Saw* as a Western. In this discussion, Williams states that 'Fenimore Cooper's noble Leatherstocking becomes the mentally sick Leatherface' and that 'Leatherstocking's Kill-Deer becomes Leatherface's chainsaw… The hunter has turned from clearing the wilderness for civilisation. He will [instead] take revenge on those who have made him obsolete, especially youthful representatives of the American family' (1996: 188).

2. While Williams sees the connections between the families through direct mirroring, Robin Wood proposes an alternative means of association when he suggests that the bickering between Cook and Hitchhiker are reflected in the teenager's 'petty malices', with Wood citing the dropping of the tooth into Pam's hand by Kirk, Jerry tormenting Franklin about Hitchhiker,

that 'Franklin resents being neglected by the others, Sally resents being burned with him' and concludes that 'the monstrous cruelties of the slaughterhouse family have their more pallid reflection within *normality*' (1979: 189–190).

3.   To compound the suggestion that *The Texas Chain Saw Massacre* can be considered to be female Gothic, Punter and Byron state that the 'Female Gothic tends to emphasise suspense rather than outright horror… it is her fears and anxieties upon which the text focuses rather than on violent encounters or rotting corpses' (2004: 279). Such a description is clearly an adequate summation of both *Chain Saws* content and style.

REFERENCES

Bould, M., 2003. Apocalypse Here and Now: Making Sense of *The Texas Chain Saw Massacre*. In: G. D. Rhodes, ed. 2003. *Horror at the Drive-in: Essays in Popular Americana.* Jefferson, N.C.: McFarland & Co. pp. 97–112.

Donaldson, L. F., 2010. Access and Excess in *The Texas Chain Saw Massacre. Movie*, [Online]. (1). Available at: http://www2.warwick.ac.uk/fac/arts/film/movie/pastissues/ [Accessed 23 March 2012]

Jaworzyn, S., 2003. *The Texas Chain Saw Massacre Companion*. London: Titan Books.

Merritt, N., 2010. Cannibalistic Capitalism and other American Delicacies: A Bataillean Taste of *The Texas Chain Saw Massacre* in *Film Philosophy Journal*, [Online]. 14 (1), Available at: http://www.film-philosophy.com/index.php/f-p/article/view/190/178 [Accessed 23 March 2012].

Punter, D. & Byron, G., 2004. *The Gothic*. Oxford: Blackwell Publishing.

Sharrett, C., 1983. The Idea of Apocalypse in *The Texas Chain Saw Massacre*. In. B. K. Grant, ed. 1984. *Planks of Reason: Essays on the Horror Film*. London: The Scarecrow Press, pp.255–276.

Williams, T., 1996. *Hearths of Darkness: The Family in the American Horror Film*. London: Associated University Presses.

Wood, R., 1979. An Introduction to the American Horror Film. In. B. K. Grant, ed. 1984. *Planks of Reason: essays on the Horror Film*. London: The Scarecrow Press, pp.164–200.

THE UNCANNY

Throughout *The Texas Chain Saw Massacre* elements of the Gothic have made themselves clearly manifest: the haunted house, the monster and sustained persecution. These tropes have provided contexts with which to address the film's content and have exposed potential readings of the text which, in the final analysis, concentrically draw themselves towards a greater concept – the uncanny. In their analysis of the recurrent elements within the Gothic, Punter and Byron suggest that the concept and occurrences of the uncanny not only forms the background to the genre but functions as the very *modus operandi* of many Gothic texts (2004: 286). With such a concept dominating the Gothic, its application to *The Texas Chain Saw* can be used to not only consolidate the proposition that the film is itself a Gothic text but, more, to draw the prior readings together and unify them in an effort to formalise a clear reading of Hooper's film.

As a concept, the uncanny was defined in Sigmund Freud's seminal essay *The Uncanny* (1919). In this text, Freud attempted to both define and understand what the uncanny was, and famously began his exploration by suggesting that some may find the idea of a psychologist engaging in such an endeavour unusual because the uncanny is primarily related to aesthetics. He quickly quells this possibility by suggesting that his research into the uncanny revealed 'virtually nothing' and found instead texts that:

> … on the whole prefer to concern themselves with our feelings for the beautiful, the grandiose and the attractive – that is to say, with feelings of a positive kind, their determinants and the objects that arouse them – rather than with their opposites, feelings of repulsion and distress. (2003: 123)

To begin his enquiry, Freud examines the etymological origins of the word. As Punter indicates, it is important to acknowledge that Freud does not explore the word 'uncanny' but instead 'the exact term which Freud is referring is not the English 'uncanny' but the German equivalent, 'unheimlich'' (2007: 130) which translates as the *unhomely*. To do this, Freud quotes (virtually in full) the entry for *heimlich* (the homely) from the 1860 edition of Daniel Sanders *Wörterbuch der Deutschen Sprache*: heimlich carries connotations of belonging to the house, of not being strange but instead being familiar, tame, dear and intimate. As the definition progresses, a shift begins to take place in that the word moves from the familiar to a sense of uncertainty as the word begins to reflect definitions of concealment, the hidden and the secret until, eventually, it comes to represent its opposite, the unheimlich. Freud concludes by stating that:

> *Heimlich* thus becomes increasingly ambivalent, until it finally merges with its antonym *unheimlich*. The uncanny (*das Unheimliche*, 'the unhomely') is in some way a species of the familiar (*das Heimliche*, 'the homely'). (2003: 134)

In this transition, the initial connections between the uncanny and the content of *The Texas Chain Saw Massacre* start to become apparent: Pam's movement from the outside of the Leatherface's house to the inside of it makes physical this shift, for its exterior is, as has been stated, an idyllic image of the rural with its brilliant white clapboard, the cooling porch, the lush green mature trees that surround the swing, all set against a deep blue sky. But once inside, when she walks through the silence and darkness of the hallway and falls into the room of feather and bone, all of what she perceived dramatically changes into its grotesque opposite – the homely exterior conceals the unhomely interior, a quality compounded by the ironic juxtaposition of the severed limbs and bones that are bound to the 'arms' and 'legs' of the furniture. In this space, the homely is transformed into a cruel parody of the normal, a frightening and grotesque perversion of what a house *should* be like.

Punter defines the shift from the *homely* to the *unhomely* as 'the crucial point' in understanding the uncanny , suggesting that the uncanny:

> … represents a feeling which relates to a dialectic between what is *known* and that which is *unknown*. If we are afraid, then more often than not it is because we are experiencing fear of the unknown: but if we have a sense of the uncanny, it is because the barriers between the known and the unknown are teetering on the brink of collapse. We are afraid, certainly; but what we are afraid of is at least partly our own sense that we have *been here before*. (2007: 130)

As Punter states, this sense of fear as a partially familiar or partially remembered experience has a predictable resonance for Freud: as his investigation continues, he works to correlate the concept of the uncanny with his psychological preoccupations and suggests that the uncanny is a form of repression:

> The uncanny is occasioned when an event in the present reminds us of something

in the (psychological) past, but something which cannot be fully remembered, a past event, situation, or feeling, which should have been locked away or buried but which has emerged to haunt the current scene. (ibid.)

For Freud, then, the uncanny is a manifestation of the past within the present and it is here, in that manifestation, that the uncanny makes a clear connection with the Gothic, for its central images – be they the haunted castle, the drifting spectre or terrifying monster – are *all* related to that central concept: as ghost or monster or even as the shadow-cast house, this return of the past generates fear in both the protagonist and reader and so suggests that, within the Gothic at least, the uncanny is the source of the genre's fearful effect, the concept by which its horror and its terror are generated. Such a proposition is supported by Freud, who having established an etymological framework for his critical investigation, continues by establishing the occurrences that stimulate the uncanny feeling:

The Double
Repetition
The inescapability of Fate
Omens, predictions, presentiments
Silence
Solitude
Darkness
Ghosts
Severed limbs and severed heads
Being buried alive
Dead bodies
Death

In this lexicon, the recurrent characters, narrative elements and events of the Gothic are clearly made manifest, giving rise to Punter and Byron's notion that 'the uncanny is [indeed] at the core of the Gothic' (2004: 286).

CHAIN SAW AS AN UNCANNY TEXT

James Marriot describes the viewing experience of *The Texas Chain Saw Massacre* as being one of 'gruelling intensity' (2007: 181). This intensity comes about not through the few graphic shocks the film contains but because of the seemingly relentless nature of the narrative events themselves, the very inexplicability of events that lead all but one of the teenagers to their untimely deaths. So sustained is this quality that Marriott compares the film to 'authentic nightmare logic' (ibid.) where events loop back upon themselves, forcing images and events to occur again and again; the emphasis upon the teenagers' distinct lack of understanding and control to the extent that it seems both have been surrendered solely to fate; all of those bad omens coming true; Pam's explanation of retrograde Saturn being visualised in the film through repeated images of the sun or moon suggesting that if fate is not in control of events, then a terrible solar alignment is. All culminate in a film which its director describes as a 'structural puzzle… the way it folds continuously back in on itself, and no matter where you're going it's the wrong place… [it's] a bad day, a cosmically bad day' (Marriott, 2007: 182).

It is perhaps obvious from the elements that make up Marriot's notion of 'authentic nightmare logic' that Freud's topos of the uncanny is made manifest. Such a connection has been alluded to throughout the chapters and need little further elucidation here: the double is found in the grotesque reflective of the Sally/Franklin and Hitchhiker/Leatherface relationship; Sally experiences a terrifying repetition of events, all of which lead her to her sustained persecution in the darkness of the cannibal family home; the solar alignments indicate that fate is clearly in control; all of those bad omens that make themselves clear to the teenagers; Pam's live burial in the freezer; the dead body at the start and all those severed body parts that litter Leatherface's house, all coupled with his decapitation of Kirk. From its very start then, *The Texas Chain Saw Massacre*'s narrative is comprised of one uncanny event after another. Sustained as it is throughout its entire narrative, it is clear that *Chain Saw* can be interpreted as a fundamentally uncanny text. But, while this may indeed be the case, it may be at the cost of not observing a further element: a nihilistic tendency that gravitates the film solely towards its central concept – death.

From the very start this quality is announced and from then on the film's imagery is purposefully constructed to ensure a complete and almost absolute destructiveness of characters and film form: the teenagers are brutally killed – two are beaten with a lump hammer, another is suspended from a hook and then frozen to death, another is disembowelled. Their murderer and his family perceives them not as people but purely as meat. Consequently, individuality and personality (even the concept of people) has been dissolved in their total rejection of 'normality'. In their sustained acts of terrorisation and murder it is clear that all formal logic, law, and order have long been abandoned and that they have instead submitted themselves to the absolute destruction of the living through the transgressive act of cannibalism. Nothing of the contemporary world is sacred to them, including the flesh and the grave. Instead, its purpose is to be destroyed so that the past – in the form of fetish objects, relics and working methods – can be resurrected, lived out, sustained, and rejoiced in.

This sense of destruction is paralleled in the film-making itself. Starting with a narration that elucidates the entire plot down to its ending, there follows a chaotic title sequence which combines grotesque imagery with abstract images, and strange and uncanny sounds with realistic radio news broadcasts. The content of certain scenes are obscured either by objects within the frame or by the distance between the camera and subject, creating a quality of frustration within the audience. Unusual angles are used throughout, as are those uncanny sounds. The narrative – what little there is of it – not only becomes a sustained scene of torture but also repeats itself time and again. Finally, the audience's expectation for the Todorovian return to equilibrium is denied, for the murderous threat survives virtually unharmed while the protagonist has descended into insanity. In essence then, *The Texas Chain Saw Massacre* does not compromise. Instead, it reduces the essential qualities of the horror film down to its most basic elements and presents them in their rawest form.

To suggest this state is to indicate that *The Texas Chain Saw Massacre* is perhaps a very *pure* horror film, a quality which correlates with the film-maker's intentions: in interview Gunnar Hansen has stated that 'people misunderstand it' for it is not, ultimately, a film about the collapse of the American family or its cannibalistic alter ego nor, as some have suggested, a reaction to the Vietnam War and the other horrors that were taking place in the US at the time. Rather, it is a film Hooper and Henkel conceived with the simple notion that they should 'take everything that ever scared [them] in a movie and put it into [what would become *Chain Saw*]' (Jaworzyn, 2003: 96). Within this set of parameters emerges Hooper's credo for horror cinema: 'the true monster is death itself' (ibid: 28). In this simple statement, genre allocation and motif are reduced down to this bare fact. By assigning death as the monster, the threat that is slowly but steadily looming upon us all is made tangible on the screen. Leatherface becomes a personification of death, his chain saw an instrument of death, the house functioning as a shrine to death, the protagonist is effectively 'dead' by the end of the film. Death isn't then just a motif within the film, it becomes a dreadful tangibility, as either an instantaneousness event (as it is with Kirk and Jerry's deaths) or a destructive protraction (as it is with Pam and seemingly so with Sally). Added to this are the deathly symbols that literally litter the film – the desecrated graves, the 'grisly work of art', the husks of bodies, all of those bones and feathers, the severed limbs, the masks of skin, the blood that stains the kitchen sink, the animal heads, the slaughterhouse, the rotting relic of the Hardesty homestead. The whole film, in virtually all of its aspect and content, is, once again, engineered towards that one singular concept – death.

DEATH

Of all the uncanny elements he identified, Freud announces that it is death that is the most uncanny of them all: 'to many people the acme of the uncanny is represented by anything to do with death' (2003: 148). In this statement Freud perhaps declares that the uncanny feeling is a concept by which the fear of death can be both articulated and understood, for death embraces all those other signifiers of the uncanny: the double signifies the death of the self; we are all fated to our own deaths; omens and predictions are (traditionally) all foretelling of deaths to come; our death is a solitary act and one which is silencing and absorbed in darkness; ghosts come back from death; the severed head is that most potent of death symbols, as are dead bodies; while to be buried alive is indeed to experience death in a suffocating darkness.

To suggest that death is the sole motif of *The Texas Chain Saw Massacre* is not to deny alternative readings of the film because, in the end, subtextual readings of the film that are aligned with culture or politics are, ultimately, grounded in the act of death themselves: the protests against Vietnam War were stimulated by the deaths on both sides – the young conscripts and, as symbol of the opposition, all those that were murdered in the My Lai Massacre – while Leatherface and his brothers were seen to mark the death of the safe and cosy image of the American family. Both are unified in the film's depiction of Americans killing Americans, violently and senselessly in an effort to adapt and survive in the face of the steady forward movement of progress. With such connections the readings of the narrative's connections with the Vietnam War become even more blatant: a group of innocent and naïve youths entire into the territory of a hostile culture, a culture which responds with brutal force when their space is invaded.

The murder of the teenagers raises a further real-world parallel through their alignment with the hippy subculture. The protagonists are clearly correlated to this social group, with Rick Worland stating that those 'kids in the van are almost reflexively understood as part of the subculture by virtue of their long hair, floral prints, and jeans alone' (2007: 214). As these characters are systematically killed, one after the other, the film unquestionably presents the death of the hippy era, as its core value of spiritual, social and sexual freedom is literally battered to death by a dark, violent and repressed force within American society. Worland reworks the idea of the teenagers being doubled by Leatherface's family by suggesting that Hitchhiker is also aligned with the hippy movement but more so with its darker, violent fringes:

> [Hitchhiker] resembles deranged cult leader Charles Manson… [and that he] personifies the threat of nihilistic violence that President Nixon's conservative 'silent majority' had come to project on the youth movement, especially after the bloody Tate-LaBianca murders in Los Angeles, just days before the Rolling Stones' free concert at Altamont Speedway ended in the murder of a fan directly in front of the stage. (ibid.)

The desired culture of freedom, it would seem in *The Texas Chain Saw Massacre*, has finally come full circle in the figure of Hitchhiker. Instead of becoming a safe social construct of life and expression, it has become a violent and untethered force that is unable to restrain or police itself. Freedom becomes violence, with expression given only in death. The events and the subtext they imply becomes apocalyptic, a psychotic drive towards total destruction.

It would seem then that from whatever perspective *Chain Saw* is considered, death is the defining parameter. With such extreme boundaries in place, the film becomes a tour de force of nihilism, an antagonistic display of the grotesque, the violent, and the deathly in a succession of increasingly disturbing images. Its chaotic and spiralling pace leads both Sally and the audience back to one space: the charnel house, that room of feather and bone, the one next to the slaughterhouse kitchen, and to the cannibals waiting at the dining table. And perhaps, in the end, that is what *The Texas Chain Saw Massacre* is *really* about: death not just as a violent and destructive force, or as the sacrosanct act of consuming flesh, but as a blunt warning to the *fate* that awaits a society that frees itself of law and order due to political and economic climates. In such unstable times, the film suggests that a family will not only defend itself with violence but support and sustain its members by any means necessary. By doing so, it frees itself of the moral, political, and economic pressures of its culture as its gives itself up to the total expression of the self.

REFERENCES

Freud, S., 2003. *The Uncanny*. London: Penguin.

Jaworzyn, S., 2003. *The Texas Chain Saw Massacre Companion*. London: Titan Books.

Marriott, J., 2007. *Horror Films*. London: Virgin Books.

Punter, D., 2007. The Uncanny. In: C. Spooner & E. McEvoy, eds. 2007. *The Routledge Companion to Gothic*. Oxon: Routledge.

Punter, D. & Byron, G., 2004. *The Gothic*. Oxford: Blackwell Publishing.

Worland, R., 2007. *The Horror Film: An Introduction*. Oxford: Blackwell Publishing.

LEGACY

Without doubt, *The Texas Chain Saw Massacre* is one of the most enduring of films of the horror genre, having attained a highly respected status from both fan and academic audiences. Its power to frighten and shock is not, in any way, diminished by its increasing age, nor is any of its visceral or brutal imagery dated in comparison to contemporary horror cinema. Such is the extent of the film's raw aggression that it has become a cornerstone of the genre, not just because of its sheer brutality but because its content, alongside George A. Romero's *Night of the Living Dead* (1968) and Wes Craven's *The Last House on the Left* (1972) irreversibly changed horror cinema: combined, these three films placed the horrific within a contemporary and recognisable America and the horror and violence that haunted that landscape was not an antiquated European monster or supernatural being but *American citizens*, people who hunted, tortured, murdered and, at times, consumed their fellow Americans. While each film offered their audiences shocking imagery (a zombie child feeding upon her mother, torture and rape, the impalement of a young woman upon a meat hook), they also reflected the times, commenting upon an America which was in throes of a significant war in Vietnam while experiencing deep civil unrest at home. Horror, it would have seemed, had literally come home.

Chain Saw has many enduring legacies, including the crew's experience of its notorious production, the financial debacle following its release and its subsequent censorship and, in some cases, outright banning. While these all have their place in the growing *mythos* of *Chain Saw*, the film's sustained impact upon the horror genre is perhaps best typified in the sustained plight of Sally, for in her experiences a new character type was potentially born – the 'Final Girl'.

SALLY, THE FINAL GIRL?

In the chapter *Her Body, Himself* in *Men, Women and Chainsaws: Gender in the Modern Horror Film* (1992), author Carol J. Clover states that Alfred Hitchcock's *Psycho* (1960) is 'the appointed ancestor' of the slasher film because of the 'unprecedented success' of a 'particular formulation' coupled with 'the sexualisation of both motive and action', which resulted in 'a flood of imitators and variations' (1992: 24). This trend would last until 1974 when *Chain Saw* was released, the point at which, Clover argues, a significant change in the slasher film took place, as Hooper's film 'revised the *Psycho* template to such a degree and in such a way as to make a new phase' (ibid.). This is primarily because *Chain Saw* (coupled with John Carpenter's seminal *Halloween* [1978]) introduced a monster 'whose only role is that of killer and one whose identity as such is clear from the outset' (ibid: 30). Whereas *Psycho*'s Norman Bates (Anthony Perkins) killed because of an uncontrollable psychosexual trauma, *Chain Saw*'s Leatherface can be read as functioning purely as a slaughtering machine, a masked killer who murders and mutilates without conscience or remorse in order to provide food for the family table.

While Bates and Leatherface may seem in opposition to each other, they are unified in some respects by a sense of transvestite behaviour. To murder, Bates must wear the wig and dress of his beloved but domineering mother and, in doing so, *becomes* her when he murders. Similarly, Leatherface wears masks[1] of female flesh that not only hide his face but, in a sense, *change* his gender and so, like Norman, he ruthlessly murders with the face of a female other. Clover indicates that Leatherface's wearing of female masks does not show 'overt signs of gender confusion' but instead a 'cathexis to the sick family' (ibid: 27) that lacks a mother figure and has, as has been previously discussed, taken on that role himself. The notion of the absent mother in the slasher film resonates throughout the subgenre from *Chain Saw* onwards: for example in *Motel Hell* (Kevin Connor, 1980), the portrait of the deceased mother is repeatedly cut to, her image continually and ambiguously looking down upon her children's incestuous and cannibalistic activity;[2] in *Friday the 13th* (Sean S. Cunningham, 1980) the killer transpires to be the actual mother and, in her murder, becomes the source of her son's endless revenge in the subsequent sequels; while in the *A Nightmare on Elm Street* (1984–2010) series, child-molester/killer Freddy Kruger's back-story is revealed as one in which his mother is a raped nun.

Possibly the most significant impact Hooper's film has had upon the horror genre is its sustained trauma of Sally Hardesty. The juxtaposition of her terrible plight but eventual survival seemingly reconfigured the genre and created, as Clover has termed it, the character of the Final Girl. Yet, for all her endurance, Sally is perhaps not the *first* Final Girl but more a survivor who stands alongside *Halloween*'s Laurie Strode (Jamie Lee

Curtis); for as much as both survive, each, in the end, requires male intervention to fully save them from the narrative's male antagonist: Sally is rescued by a passing driver, while Laurie is saved by Dr Loomis (Donald Pleasance). Despite this, both Sally and Laurie combine to make manifest the key attributes of the Final Girl as both struggled, endured and, in Laurie's case, attacked their aggressor until they could escape and be saved. In the slasher films that followed in the wake of *Chain Saw* and *Halloween*, the Final Girl steadily gains in strength until she herself vanquishes the male antagonist. It is this that prevents Sally from being a true Final Girl, for she (unlike Laurie and all the others that followed) never turns upon her aggressors and attacks *them*. Instead, she simply endures, runs from them and, by chance, seizes an opportunity to escape. However, this is not to disagree with Clover's positioning of Sally as a Final Girl, as she does indeed endure and it is this that makes her so noteworthy. Clover comments that the violent experiences endured by the Final Girl will occupy between the last ten to twenty minutes of the slasher film but makes special note that Sally's Final Girl sequence is approximately thirty minutes in duration. Sally survives by running, evading, and attempted bargaining until the opportunity to escape arises. Until then, she is tormented, beaten, tortured, repeatedly hit with a hammer and sliced open, yet she never really gives up and, in the end, with what remains of her strength she does indeed escape.

With such a sustained and prolonged agony for the character, it is perhaps not to problematic to suggest then that apart from Sally being a proto Final Girl, *The Texas Chain Saw Massacre* is itself a prototype for the recently emerged trend of Torture Porn: appearing in the early part of the 21st century, this sub-genre of films places great emphasis on the confinement and subsequent explicit torture of (usually female) victims. These violent assaults are shown on-screen as a form of both shocking image and titillation, yet they do not provide a catharsis for the audience in the escape of those being tortured. Instead, the audience must endure as the fictional characters do and then continue to watch as these people die horrific deaths. While Chain Saw finally allowed Sally to escape, *Hostel* (Eli Roth, 2005), *Wolf Creek* (Greg Mclean, 2005), *Turistas* (John Stockwell, 2006), *Hostel Part 2* (Eli Roth, 2007) and *Captivity* (Roland Joffe, 2007) all revel in bodily assault, disfiguration and murder. While critical reaction to these films was generally negative, audiences were drawn to this new type of film and, subsequently, made torture porn films profitable: *Hostel* had a budget of less than $5 million and went on to gross over $80 million. Ironically, the dominion of torture porn at the box office would be usurped by the emergence of the horror film remake, in particular with the franchise 'reboot' of *The Texas Chain Saw Massacre*.

THE TEXAS CHAIN SAW MASSACRE: THE SEQUELS

Given the success of *Chain Saw*, a sequel was perhaps inevitable. According to Stefan Jaworzyn, 'in the 1970s Warren Skaaren and Bill Parsley had acquired the rights... but Skaaren's script draft script thankfully remained unproduced' (2003: 128). The sequel would eventually be released in 1986, having been co-produced and directed by Hooper for Cannon Films: Hooper signed a three-picture deal with Cannon's owners, Menahem Golan and Yoram Globus, first making *Space Vampires* (1985) (to be later titled *Lifeforce*) and then *Invaders from Mars* (1986) before completing the deal with *Chain Saw 2*. In an interview with Keith Phipps (2000), Hooper states that he was originally only slated to produce the sequel but as he couldn't 'find anyone my budget would afford, a director whose work I knew' (ibid: 149), he ended up directing the film himself. With Hooper now directing, it was assumed the surviving characters and their actors would also return but only Jim Siedow would return to reprises his role of Cook.

With Hitchhiker dead and Sally escaped, the sequel takes place many years after the events of the first film. Leatherface and his family have remained active for this period but find their way of life threatened with the arrival of Lieutenant 'Lefty' Enright (Dennis Hopper), a former Texas Ranger and the uncle of Sally and Franklin Hardesty. He has spent the time between the films investigating his cousin's murder and soon finds the cannibal family home where, armed with multiple chain saws, begins to exact his revenge.

Although clearly a sequel – of sorts – by virtue of its narrative and reappearance of certain characters from the original, *The Texas Chain Saw Massacre 2* is also very much its own film in terms of its approach to realism, on-screen violence and black comedy. Whereas the original was subdued in these aspects, the sequel takes full advantage of a standard film budget to create lavish and violent special effects (executed by horror icon, Tom Savini) and to amplify the thick strain of humour that runs through its narrative. As a consequence, the intense realism and slow, brooding build-up of tension present within the first film is replaced with gore-soaked set-pieces and scenes of stark humour, all of which dispel any sense of tension the film may have been creating. As Hooper has himself commented, the released film was a product of his 'frustration at the comedy in the first film not being appreciated or understood' and he likes the sequel:

> … as a wacky, crazy, bizarre, over-the-top dark comedy, but it missed its mark in doing what the audience expected it to do, which was to scare the hell out of them and give them a little more of what they experienced in the first film… It was part of a deal commitment, and I had fun doing it to the detriment of the film itself. (ibid: 169)

Despite these reservations, *Chain Saw 2* contains some shocking scenes, most notably those involving the female character Stretch (Caroline Williams): as a local radio DJ, Stretch gets involved in Lefty's investigations and is soon attacked by Leatherface who, having cornered her in the radio station, places his chain saw between her legs and up against her crotch. While licking his lips, Leatherface rocks slowly back and forth in a simulation of either masturbation or sexual intercourse. As he reaches his climax, Leatherface moves the saw away and revs it yet, in a moment of the film's dark sense of humour, the chain saw misfires. In his frustration at not being able to reach a climax, Leatherface screams and pulls frantically at the saw's ignition cord until it eventually fires. By now Stretch has hidden herself and watches as Leatherface proceeds to saw his way through the various objects and structures in the room in which she hides. A more horrific scene involves Stretch being made to wear the recently flayed face of a co-worker and then engage in a chain saw confrontation with Leatherface's (other) brother, the insane Chop Top (Bill Moseley). This sequence correlates with Sally's escape in the original as Chop Top (who is effectively replaying the role of Hitchhiker) repeatedly slashes at Stretch's back with a cut-throat razor, just as Hitchhiker does to Sally as she runs down the driveway to the presumed safety of the road. The confrontation ends with Stretch slashing open Chop Top's stomach (mirroring Leatherface slashing open his own leg in the original) and pushing him over a cliff face to his death. Having killed him, Stretch stands with her chain saw held aloft, swinging it around and around her head, screaming and dancing in a manner no different to that of Leatherface's insane ritualistic dance at the end of *The Texas Chain Saw Massacre*. In this mirrored ending, Stretch may be Clover's Final Girl but she exits the narrative just as insane as her predecessor, Sally.

Following *Texas Chain Saw Massacre 2* were two further entries in the original franchise: *Leatherface: Texas Chain Saw Massacre 3* (Jeff Burr, 1989) and *The Texas Chain Saw Massacre: The Next Generation* (Kim Henkel, 1994). Neither did particularly well at the box office and are perhaps more notable for their cast, with *Chain Saw 3* starring Viggo Mortensen (as Tex) and Ken Foree (as Benny) while *The Next Generation* stars a young Rene Zellweger (as Jenny) and Matthew McConaughey (as Vilmer) and a cameo appearance from Marilyn Burns as a character simply identified as 'Patient on Gurney' in the credits.

THE TEXAS CHAIN SAW MASSACRE: THE REMAKE

Nine years after *The Next Generation*, the original *Texas Chain Saw Massacre* was remade as part of a series of genre remakes produced by Michael Bay's Platinum Dunes production company. The series, to date, includes *The Amityville Horror* (Andrew Douglas, 2005), *The Hitcher* (David Meyers, 2007), *Friday the 13th* (Marcus Nispel, 2009) and *A Nightmare on Elm Street* (Samuel Bayer, 2010). While ostensibly marketed as a remake, this film is actually a significant reworking of Hooper and Henkel's original. This *Chain Saw*, directed by Marcus Nispel (2003) uses only key elements from the original and reworks them into a different narrative and, as a consequence, introduces new characters that rework or, perhaps more appropriately, rewrite the background history to Leatherface's family. More significantly, this version of the film provides a depth of character to Leatherface that wasn't evident in the original, by giving him a name – Thomas Brown Hewitt – a defined childhood and a clear reason for his wearing the masks of flayed faces – a debilitating skin disease which has caused his facial features to rot. In these changes, Leatherface shifts from the lumbering, anonymous and ambiguous killer of the original to a *person defined*. In this transition the raw horror of Leatherface is dissolved. He is no longer a sheer force, the mute figure of insanity and violence that cannot be reasoned with (or even understood) but a character with a name and a past; a voice.

In this respect, it is perhaps better to consider Nispel's *Chain Saw* as a stand-alone film and one to be considered upon its own merits. As a contemporary horror film, this *Chain Saw Massacre* is predictably stylish and composed – the images Nispel creates of the American landscape are both beautiful and resonant, an environment baking in a hazy heat and one drained of colour – with the sort of stunningly graphic set-pieces that modern audiences have come to expect from horror films. Typifying both of these elements is the film's reworking of the sequence in which the original teenagers pick up Hitchhiker: in the remake, the group pick up a girl who they see stumbling down the roadside. Once in the van, it becomes apparent she is in a state of shock and, before the teenagers can help her, she produces a handgun from in between her legs, opens her mouth, and shoots herself. The sequence is both graphic and stylised: not only is her suicide gorily depicted on screen but, immediately following her death, the camera literally travels through the hole in her skull, out through the shattered rear window of the vehicle and out into the beautiful, desaturated landscape. Such a scene makes clear that this is not just a remake or a reworking but an entirely different film in terms of content, style and production values. Whereas Hooper had a minimal budget, Nispel had $9.5 million (although still a low budget by contemporary standards); whereas Hooper opts for a slow and steady build-up of tension, Nispel orchestrates fear through one gory and graphic set piece after another; where Hooper's film was drenched in an atmosphere of filth and degradation, Nispel's film has a polished patina that makes even the most graphically gory of scenes look beautiful.

Nispel's film is, in its own right, skilfully made and imbued with scenes of significant tension and horror; yet, ironically, it remains the complete opposite of its source material. In its very polish and professionalism it is a world away from Hooper's rough-and-ready fever dream, the original *Texas Chain Saw Massacre*.

ENDNOTES

1. Leatherface's use of the mask would be later replicated in a number of slasher films, most notably in *Halloween*, *Friday the 13th* and more recently in the *Scream* (Wes Craven, 1996–2011) series of films.

2. Clover also footnotes (1992: 25) that the cannibalistic aspects of some slashers find their potential point of origin in *Chain Saw*, with Hooper's film clearly suggesting that the sausages

that sizzle away in Cook's grill in the garage are not made of pork or beef but the flesh of those who have been caught and butchered by Hitchhiker and Leatherface. The notion that innocent urbanites would unknowingly eat human flesh finds its zenith in *Motel Hell* and in Hooper's sequel *The Texas Chain Saw Massacre 2* (1986).

REFERENCES

Clover, C. J., 1999. *Men, Women and Chainsaws*, New Jersey: Princeton University Press.

Jaworzyn, S., 2003. *The Texas Chain Saw Massacre Companion*, London: Titan Books.

GENERAL BIBLIOGRAPHY

Becker, M., 2006. 'A Point of Little Hope: Hippie Horror Films and the Politics of Ambivalence', in *The Velvet Light Trap*, No. 57, Spring 2006, pp. 42–59.

Brighton, L., 1975. 'Saturn in Retrograde or the Texas Jump Cut', in *Film Journal*, Vol. 2, no. 4, pp. 24–27.

Brottman. M., 1997. *Offensive Films: Toward an Anthropology of Cinema Vomitif.* Westport: Greenwood Press.

Curtis, B., 2008. *Dark Places: The Haunted House in Film*. London: Reakiton Books.

Dudenhoffer, L., 2008. 'Monster Mishmash: Iconicity and Intertextuality in Tobe Hooper's *The Texas Chain Saw Massacre*', in *Journal of the Fantastic in the Arts*, Vol. 19, no. 1, pp. 51–69.

Fawver, K., 2011 'Massacres of Meaning: The Semiotic Value of Silence and Scream in *The Texas Chain Saw Massacre* and *Halloween*', in *The Irish Journal of Gothic and Horror Studies* [Online], no. 10, October 2011, Available at: http://irishgothichorrorjournal.homestead. com/Fawver.html [Accessed 23 March 2012].

Hill, D., 2010. '*The Texas Chain Saw Massacre*', in J. Berra, ed. 2010. *Directory of World Cinema: The American Independents*. Bristol: Intellect Books. pp. 81–83.

Jones, M., 2002. 'Head Cheese: *The Texas Chain Saw Massacre* Beyond Leatherface', in X. Mendik, ed. 2002. *Shocking Cinema of the Seventies*. Hereford: Noir Publishing. pp. 178–192.

Langford, B., 2005. *Film Genre: Hollywood and Beyond*. Edinburgh: Edinburgh University Press.

Muir, J. K., 2002. *Eaten Alive at a Chain Saw Massacre: The Films of Tobe Hooper*. Jefferson: McFarland.

Sharrett, C., 1983. 'The Idea of Apocalypse in *The Texas Chain Saw Massacre*', in B. K. Grant, ed. 1996. *Planks of Reason: Essays on the Horror Film*. Lanham: Scarecrow Press.

DEVIL'S ADVOCATES

"Auteur Publishing's new Devil's Advocates critiques on individual titles offer bracingly fresh perspectives from passionate writers. The series will perfectly complement the BFI archive volumes." Christopher Fowler, Independent on Sunday

LET THE RIGHT ONE IN — ANNE BILLSON

"Anne Billson offers an accessible, lively but thoughtful take on the '80s-set Swedish vampire belter... a fun, stimulating exploration of a modern masterpiece." Empire

WITCHFINDER GENERAL — IAN COOPER

"I enjoyed it very much; it sets out all the various influences, both before and after the film, and indeed the essence of the film itself, very well indeed." Jonathan Rigby, author of English Gothic

SAW — BENJAMIN POOLE

"This is a great addition to a series of books that are starting to become compulsory for horror fans. It will also help you to appreciate just what an original and amazing experience the original SAW truly was." The Dark Side

THE TEXAS CHAIN SAW MASSACRE — JAMES ROSE

"[James Rose] find[s] new and unusual perspectives with which to address [the] censor-baiting material. Unsurprisingly, the effect... is to send the reader back to the films... watch the films, read these Devil's Advocate analyses of them." Crime Time

Printed and bound by CPI Group (UK) Ltd, Croydon, CR0 4YY

13/04/2025

14656594-0001